FREQUENTLY ASKED

WHITE
QUESTIONS

AJAY PARASRAM + ALEX KHASNABISH

Development editing: Fazeela Jiwa
Copyediting: Erin Seatter
Cover design: Jess Koroscil
Design and layout: Jess Koroscil

Printed and bound in Canada

Published by Fernwood Publishing
2970 Oxford Street, Halifax, Nova Scotia, B3L 2W4
and 748 Broadway Avenue, Winnipeg, Manitoba, R3G 0X3
fernwoodpublishing.ca

Fernwood Publishing Company Limited gratefully acknowledges the financial support of the Government of Canada through the Canada Book Fund and the Canada Council for the Arts. We acknowledge the Province of Manitoba for support through the Manitoba Publishers Marketing Assistance Program and the Book Publishing Tax Credit. We acknowledge the Province of Nova Scotia through the Publishers Assistance Fund.

   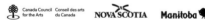

Library and Archives Canada Cataloguing in Publication
Title: Frequently asked white questions / by Ajay Parasram and Alex Khasnabish.
Names: Parasram, Ajay, author. | Khasnabish, Alex, 1976- author.
Description: Includes bibliographical references and index.
Identifiers: Canadiana (print) 20220259739 | Canadiana (ebook) 2022025981X
ISBN 9781773635576 (softcover)
ISBN 9781773635781 (EPUB)
ISBN 9781773635798 (PDF)
Subjects: LCSH: White people—Race identity—Miscellanea.
LCSH: Race relations—Miscellanea. | LCSH: Race—Miscellanea.
Classification: LCC HT1575 .P37 2022 | DDC 305.809—dc23

CONTENTS

FOR FAWQ'S SAKE

Recently, Ajay facilitated an antiracism workshop as part of a youth activism conference, during which a Black student was explaining why she felt degraded, angry, and hurt when white people use the n-word. In his effort to express empathy with her, a young white man in the circle used the n-word several times. Many white people in the room were loudly outraged that the young man had used this word, while others seemed confused as to why so much time was being spent on a word. Ajay and the Black student who had spoken looked at each other. She seemed tired, but neither angry nor surprised. The young white man shrunk into his chair and said nothing else for the rest of the workshop.

He was not trying to be an asshole. But he was not adequately prepared to have a conversation about race at the same level as another person his age, someone navigating life as a Black woman. Because he was not prepared, what should have been a great experience for everyone in the room ended up being another example of a racialized person servicing a predominantly white group by sharing their lived experience and gaining nothing from the ordeal. In this context, the white group did more than just correct the white guy for using the n-word; they were able to perform outrage, signalling their progressive credentials. As is typical in situations of white privilege, the feelings, desires, and sentiments of the racialized woman experiencing the racist aggression (unintended as it was) were used only as fuel for a conversation about and between white people.

And that young white guy? We have no idea what he is up to now, but if he walked out of that workshop feeling ashamed or angry or confused, he likely will not walk back into a space like that soon. It's not far-fetched to think he may have been attracted to a gathering facilitated by people who promote slogans like "It's okay to be white," which happened at Alex's university around the same time. White nationalism is rising in Canada, and white nationalist organizers are clever about how they frame their messages to attract impressionable people.

It's unfair to nonwhite participants in public or educational sessions to have to offer both training and emotional support to the white people around them, as education professor Robin DiAngelo has outlined clearly in her work on the subject of white fragility. It's also unfair to expect white people to understand the politics of race when the very operation of racial politics in Canada has encouraged them to not think or talk about race lest they appear to be racist.

● ● ●

White nationalism, *noun*
A political ideology that views white people as a distinct group and calls for the creation of white ethnostates through the expulsion of nonwhite people, often through violent means.

This is one of the fundamental challenges in offering antiracist education: white people have been organized over several generations to ignore race, to be "colourblind." People who are not white have also been told to forget about race, given the great racial equality battles of the twentieth century are allegedly over (e.g., desegregation struggles, including Viola Desmond sitting in the whites-only section of a Nova Scotian theatre; movements against explicit racial discrimination such as the Chinese head tax, Japanese internment, the *Komagata Maru* incident, and the destruction of Africville; and associated movements for reparations for colonialism). The message has been that if racial equality has been achieved, then to even think in racial terms at all is to *be racist*. However, the conference example above and many instances like it make clear that people need to talk about race if they want to converse and live equitably with each other. Some level of extra help was necessary to get that white male — and those who were quick to performatively condemn him, along with those who thought the n-word was not such a big deal — to understand the politics of race in this country before he could respectfully respond to a Black woman sharing her thoughts.

This experience, paired with a host of similar experiences at public events, work, and in our personal lives, brought Ajay and Alex together over an exceptionally hoppy beverage late in 2019. We wanted to think hard about how we could use our privileges as teachers and researchers to help take the burden of educating white people off racialized people. We also wanted to encourage a practice space for white people to deepen their knowledge of race and social justice issues without fear of conflict. By talking candidly about race, which is uncomfortable for so many white people, we wanted to proactively prevent them from being welcomed into the waiting arms of white nationalists.

So we hosted a drop-in session called *Safe Space for White Questions* (SSFWQ) in February 2020 at Dalhousie University. The premise was to ask us any question related to race and we would have a nonjudgmental conversation about it. The small in-person event included good discussions about how to teach Black poetry if you are white, how to navigate power relations within the workplace, and more. We envisioned hosting monthly sessions, ideally off-campus, but then in March 2020 COVID-19 put everything on hold. We started again online in September 2020, which had the added benefit of allowing people to pose questions anonymously, and we got a lot of engagement. By December 2020, Fernwood Publishing took notice of the project and volunteered to run the tech for us. We've been recording monthly online drop-in sessions ever since.

SSFWQ has been cultivated mostly with well-intentioned white people in mind, but it has always been open to anyone who wants to pop in and ask a question they might not want to pose in public or with family and friends. The objectives of the sessions are both educational and political. Educational, because the work of understanding how race operates simply has a lot to do with information that is not easy to access and interpret. Political, because we want to help build racial resilience among all people as a way to build equitable relations; we believe providing practice space for white people to work through racial issues might help them engage confidently and respectfully in public conversations with other white and racialized people in their lives. Calling it a "safe space" has drawn some reasonable criticism, as the concept of safe space was originated several decades ago by queer and Black organizers, who made the point that all spaces were inherently hetero and white. So it's controversial to use the phrase for white people, who are generally safe everywhere they go, in institutions and spaces that have been built by them, for them. Still, we see it as a reasonable borrow from the long tradition of activism that helps to produce social change, and as a cheeky indictment of the fact that most white people who bemoan the existence of safe spaces for racialized people need a space of their own to discuss relatively basic issues about race.

Frequently Asked White Questions (FAWQ) draws on ten recurring themes that run through questions people ask during SSFWQ episodes. We wrote this book because in reflecting on the discussions we've had over the last two years of running the show, we noticed patterns in the causes of anxiety and trepidation for white people who genuinely want to deepen their understanding of racial issues without creating more stress for the racialized people in their lives.

We want this book to be an easy and helpful read for anyone who needs a baseline from which to better understand race. We use Canadian examples wherever possible, as this context tends to be eclipsed by the racial politics of the United States. However, we understand that nation-states are not neat containers, and the politics of race is as much a global phenomenon as it is context specific — something we talk more about in the rest of the book.

While we both study race, racism, white nationalism, and white supremacy in our paid gigs as university professors, we are not especially interested in an academic approach for this book. More than a hundred years of detailed, meticulous, and groundbreaking academic scholarship on race demonstrates how structural white supremacy is the foundation for modern society — but most people will never read that work. A lot of it is published behind academic paywalls and written in technical language, making it decidedly less accessible to those outside the university. More importantly, most of the work by racialized activists and scholars is concerned primarily with the cause of achieving freedom and liberation for their people. In other words, white people are not necessarily the target audience for much of this work. We think it's crucial that white people learn about the way race affects their lives too. We see this as supporting all of that liberatory work by and for racialized people.

Compounding the issue, in recent years a resurgent right wing around the world has been working to destroy public confidence in scholarly research and evidence. In the United States, our colleagues are being attacked by democratically elected legislators for the crime

● ● ●

Racialized, *adjective / verb*
To be categorized and integrated into society's racial hierarchy based on one's perceived race. The implication is that something is being done to racialize a person; they do not naturally exist in a state of "race." Whiteness is a racial identity as well, but because it is at the top of the racial hierarchy people who are white or white-passing rarely understand themselves in racial terms.

White supremacy, *noun*
The belief that white people not only constitute a distinct people in racial and ethnic terms but are superior to nonwhite people. Institutions and states can be white supremacist based on foundational, historical structures that continue to exist today, even if they are not explicitly run by white supremacists.

of studying and teaching "critical race theory," a term used colloquially to describe any serious engagement with race in society. According to Rashawn Ray and Alexandra Gibbons from the Brookings Institute, Fox News said the phrase "critical race theory" 1,300 times between August and November 2021.[1] By that November, when Ray and Gibbons wrote their article, nine US states had passed legislation effectively banning critical race theory from schools and another twenty had similar kinds of legislation in the works.

Critical race theory, along with words like "intersectionality," is a lightning rod for white people who believe our society is already free and equal. Whether the charge is "cancel culture" or "social justice warriors" allegedly destroying the fabric of modern civilization by removing statues or renaming streets, we take up these concerns throughout the book. In some important ways, critical race theory and intersectionality are tools with which to build the world that many middle- and upper-class straight white men think they already live in.

To the casual observer, it may seem like the pushback against social justice came about during the reign of former US president Donald Trump, but this is a nearsighted view. The resurgence of the right is much older than Trump; he was preceded internationally by career politicians including Indian prime minister Narendra Modi and Filipino president Rodrigo Duterte. The very important and still incremental gains made recently in Western countries, including talking about racism as a real thing and beginning to reckon publicly with ongoing colonial violence, have been met by an overwhelming response from right-wing white nationalists. They have done an exemplary job of producing easy-to-consume propaganda to convince people that "social justice warriors" or "postmodern neo-Marxists" are trying to destroy all that is good and sacred in this world. Those who have power have always resisted changing the structures that give them power. Beneficiaries of unearned power and privilege (e.g., a trust fund kid who never had to work three part-time jobs while going to school) are especially vocal about defending society as it is rather than supporting changes to make it fairer for everyone.

One of the best ways to understand forms of oppression is learning the difference between agents and structures. We return to this point throughout the book's chapters, because like the proverbial chicken and egg, it's not about which one creates the other but rather how the two re-create one another in practice. We may not always be explicit about structure and agent, but you can keep score as you read and see how many times you can catch us explaining structure and agent in different ways!

● ● ●

Agents and structures, *noun*
Society is composed of agents, or individuals, who are part of many kinds of structures, or institutions. A structure can refer to a place, like a parliament, or it can refer to a form of social power, such as heterosexuality. Agents are embedded within structures in any given society, and structures shape people's understanding of what is "normal." At the same time, structures can shift and transform as a result of pressure exerted by agents within them.

Populism, *noun*
An approach to politics that emphasizes the interests of "the people" over those of the elites who exercise control in society. It can take the form of right-wing populism, as seen with former US president Donald Trump and Canadian politicians Maxime Bernier and Pierre Poilievre, or left-wing populism, as exemplified by the late Venezuelan president Hugo Chavez.

We wrote FAWQ to confront the rising tide of white nationalism and right-wing populism. We also wrote it because our students, friends, comrades, and fellow travellers have asked for a straight-to-the-point analysis they can recommend to people in their lives who are not interested in dense theory. Ultimately, we wrote this book because we believe helping white people understand race helps everyone build the kind of world we deserve and urgently need. If you want to learn more about racial justice but do not want to overburden your nonwhite friends with questions, this book is for you. If you feel shy or intimidated by not knowing the right lingo to use without inadvertently offending someone, this book is for you. If you struggle to find the words to help your peers or loved ones understand how race and economic justice go together, this book is for you. And if you are just damn tired of having to explain things to people who seem convinced the only way to understand something is to play devil's advocate, we hope this book can offer you some reprieve as well.

Without further ado, here are the top ten most frequently asked white questions we get:

- Can you be racist against white people?
- How do we fix past wrongs without creating new ones?
- How does racism relate to other forms of oppression?
- How can I make antiracism part of my family life?
- How can I talk about social justice without turning people off?
- What's the difference between cultural appreciation and cultural appropriation?

- Can members of an oppressed group be oppressors?
- How can white people be involved in antiracist struggles without centring themselves?
- How can I be an antiracist in my everyday life?
- How can we build the world we deserve?

Each question is addressed in a chapter, and the chapters are all deliberately short. Within each of these thematic questions, we explore different facets of frequently asked white questions that overlap with one another in ways we hope you will find mutually reinforcing as you read. At the conclusion of each chapter, we distill its main point, and at the end of book is a compilation of the top ten principles for thinking about racial politics as a white person. We take time to define important terms, which form the glossary at the end of the book. And in case you are interested in reading more, alongside our references for this book is the reading list we have kept over two years of answering questions during SSFWQ.

We hope you will engage with this book, share it with your friends and family, fight about it, disagree with it, and ultimately get some use of it.

CAN YOU BE RACIST AGAINST WHITE PEOPLE?

If racism is about discriminating against identifiable groups of people, aren't white people also victims of racism? This is a question we get a lot. It's a prickly one too. Do jokes about white people's inability to dance, terms like "white trash" or "redneck," and popular skewering of "Karens" and "Kens" amount to antiwhite racism? Why can other ethnic or racialized groups call for "pride" and "power" but when white people do that it's seen as white supremacy? Are hiring initiatives prioritizing racialized applicants just a form of racism in reverse? (Comedian Aamer Rahman explains the misplaced idea of "reverse racism" better than we ever could, so put down the book and search the internet for that clip — you won't be disappointed).

At a purely superficial level, it seems like these questions mirror the racist logic that racialized people and their allies have struggled against for so long. But just like context is the only way to tell whether someone is winking at you or just blinking, racism is also about context. White people's lives can certainly be hard, but in a society structured by white supremacy, none of those lives are hard because of their whiteness. Understanding why this is true is a little like peeling an onion: we're dealing with layers. The purpose of this chapter is to work our way down through these layers to a better understanding of racism, how and why it works, and why it's not possible, at this moment in history, to be racist against white people.

Racism's First Layer

To understand who is and isn't a victim of racism requires clarity about what racism is. Racism is a system of oppressive social relations rooted in the false belief that humanity can be divided into distinct and unequal groups based on arbitrary observable characteristics like skin colour, with implications for who counts as fully human and who does not. Just to be clear, there is an absolute mountain of evidence in fields like genetics and paleoarchaeology that proves the utterly nonsensical nature of modern racial categories.[2] Genetically speaking, there is no such thing as race. We might say race is a biological fiction but a social fact. It does not make any sense as a legitimate biological category, but it matters deeply in society.

● ● ●

Racism, *noun*
A system of oppressive social relations rooted in the false belief that humanity can be divided into distinct and unequal groups based on arbitrary observable characteristics such as skin colour, with implications for who counts as fully human and who does not.

There is no scientific basis for the division of humans into distinct and separate species. In fact, genetic science tells us there is more variation within so-called racial groups than there is between them. Human variation is a vast gradient, not an either/or choice. Skin colour is an extremely changeable feature of our human biology and is certainly no more or less significant from a genetic perspective than height, eye colour, or whether our earwax is wet or dry. But certain characteristics, and particularly skin tone, have been made very meaningful from a social perspective.

Some say racism is a natural, if regrettable, outcome of the human need to categorize the world. It's actually a relatively recent development shaped by power dynamics at work in different contexts. Racism as we know it today is a belief system cobbled together over time, not something that sprung into the world fully formed. It has not stalked humanity through the primordial mists of evolutionary history. So where did it come from?

Racism's Second Layer

Modern racism arose during the Western European interimperial scramble for other people's land, labour, and wealth, which began some five hundred years ago.[3] In essence, racism provided the justification for dispossessing other people of their territory, resources, and self-determination without falling afoul of Christian morals prohibiting murder, theft, and other forms of antisocial behaviour. After all, killing, enslaving, and stealing from other people was clearly wrong — but what if these other people were not actually people?

Racism furnished the necessary justifications as the age of imperialism, colonialism, and capitalism unfolded, and it did so even against the backdrop of the Western European Scientific Revolution and Enlightenment. Those inhabiting the imperial centres (white Western Europeans) were positioned at the top of the racial ladder, while everyone else was arrayed on rungs below depending on how closely they conformed to the civilizational standard of whiteness.[4] In essence, whiteness became a key marker of full humanity and civilizational progress. While racism has shapeshifted over time in terms of how it looks (slavery, lynchings, and segregation before; police killings of racialized people, dehumanizing memes, and vast inequalities in wealth and health now), the underlying principle of a racial hierarchy with white people at the top has not. By this fact alone, it's impossible to be racist against white people in a context of globalized white supremacy.

• • •

Imperialism, *noun*
The process of one people expanding their power to rule over other peoples and places. It involves the extension of economic, political, and social domination of one group over another using tools ranging from diplomacy to military force.

Colonialism, *noun*
The process of one people establishing control over another people and their territory with the aim of securing enduring relations of exploitation.

Capitalism, *noun*
An economic system and ideology based on the production of commodities for sale on the market in pursuit of profit. Under this system, workers must sell their labour in exchange for a wage to survive.

Racism's Third Layer

Now we are really peeling back the layers of racism, but we have deeper yet to go.

Let's be clear: White people can experience oppression due to other aspects of their identity such as gender, sexuality, age, or ability. Whiteness also does not prevent people from being exploited. The act of living off someone else's labour is exploitation. All workers in capitalist societies are exploited because the central motivating force of the capitalist economy is not meeting human needs but generating profits for the owning class. Profit is the gap between how much something cost to make and how much it is sold for. Seems simple enough, but where does this gap come from? While owners can invest in all kinds of tools, infrastructure, and other efficiencies in producing whatever it is they sell (food, cars, smartphones, jeans, litter boxes, etc.), extracting maximum productivity from workers for minimum pay is the most lucrative source of profit. All workers who have to sell their labour to survive under capitalism are exploited.

However, people are not all targeted by the same oppressions, because their identities are different and are set in a social world that has context and history. Racism is not individuals having bad thoughts and feelings about other people; it is the foundational belief in a hierarchy of human groups that sets the stage for how members of these groups are treated in society. Racism, like any social relation, lives in society. It is not an abstract concept or a game of hypothetical situations. This is why history matters: it is the soil in which society grows.

Centring this history is imperative in order to make sense of the challenges and opportunities that confront society today. Some groups have been considered more human than others, more entitled not only to make decisions about the lives of others but to dispose of those people and their lives as they see fit. For example, until the 1950s in Canada, Indigenous people living on-reserve were unable to leave without securing a pass from the Indian agent, a position staffed overwhelmingly by white men who could issue or deny a pass at their discretion. That made the ability of an Indigenous person to move around dramatically different from that of a white settler. Maybe that white settler had terrible life experiences otherwise. Maybe they were dehumanized in their job, exploited, treated shabbily by their boss, a victim of violence on the street. All those things can be true. Still, simply by virtue of their racialized identity, they were not in the same place as another person who is legally and structurally discriminated against by the system.

Whiteness as a category of being is deeply tied to how the capitalist ruling class has striven to ensure working people do not achieve a broad solidarity capable of challenging and changing the status quo.[5] If workers see each other as competitors and even racial enemies, they are unlikely to find common cause. At the same time, the social

---

Ruling class, *noun*
The strata of individuals in a society who exercise the greatest power over others. Under capitalism the owners of the means of production make up the ruling class.

and psychological comforts of not being at the very bottom of the social ladder have been dangled in front of workers who could identify as white, shielding them from some of the worst outcomes of the status quo and buying their compliance. Racism and its relationship to whiteness must be thought about in this context. In societies that are fragments of the process of Western European colonization, it is functionally impossible to be racist against white people because the origin story of these societies is inextricably tied to white supremacy, which has been encoded in the laws, norms, and values of these societies.

If you are attentive to and curious about the world around us, it's dispiritingly easy to see examples of structural white supremacy and its consequences for racialized people. For example, according to a report authored by criminologist Scot Wortley, in Halifax Black people are six times more likely than white people to be stopped, identified, and questioned by police under the practice of supposedly random street checks.[6] Young Black men are particularly likely to be stopped and questioned by police, a racialized disparity that cannot be accounted for by any other factor. It's not useful to understand this problem as the actions of a few individually racist cops. In a context of structural white supremacy, the issue is not the behaviour or beliefs of individuals at all. The issue is the way social relations and institutions are structured to produce the effects they do.

Prevailing power relations shape who is seen as a threat to social order and what is to be done about them. For example, since 2010 white supremacist terrorism has accounted for three-quarters of all domestic terror killings in Canada and the United States. Despite white men being overwhelmingly responsible for these attacks, this group has not been identified by politicians, law enforcement, or policymakers as a public threat. No one has suggested a military occupation of white-majority countries. No one has said white men represent an existential threat to civilization, democracy, or freedom. No one has suggested surveilling social, religious, and political contexts that white men frequent.

Contrast this to the rhetoric and actions following terrorist attacks carried out by Islamic fundamentalist militants. White men who commit grotesque acts of public violence are treated as unique individuals struggling with a variety of life circumstances and perhaps mental illness. Their actions are frequently explained as the result of having come to a breaking point because of some frustration or disappointment they faced. Racialized people who commit similar acts are seen as avatars of their racial group whose actions should be understood as part of a conspiracy or existential threat to Western civilization itself.

Examples of this kind of racialized differential treatment are legion. The American Revolution — a revolt of white, slave-owning, propertied men against another group of white, slave-owning, propertied men — is generally heralded as a great revolution. The Haitian Revolution, in which enslaved Africans liberated themselves from the yoke of French and British domination, culminating in the first free Black republic in the world, is not only excluded from the pantheon of great revolutions but often cast as an atrocity.

It's impossible to come up with an example of a context where white people have been systematically dispossessed, disenfranchised, and dehumanized *as white people* in the same way that racialized people have experienced. Some point to the plight of the Irish in the early days of the United States, but this example only proves the point about racialized inequity: the Irish were regarded as degraded whites and had to prove their whiteness, which they did by distancing themselves from and antagonizing other racialized groups. They were deployed against Black people with the explicit intent of putting down Black freedom struggles. Irish immigrants fleeing famine and arriving in the United States in the mid-nineteenth century routinely voted for pro-slavery politicians, publicly opposed the abolition of slavery, and engaged in routine street violence against Black and Chinese people.[7] Irish Americans were not intrinsically predisposed to anti-Black hate; they coveted whiteness, which would entitle them to political rights and jobs. Being willing and able to enact violence against other oppressed people won the Irish inclusion, however partially, in white society.

As these examples illustrate, while it's certainly possible for white people to suffer, be exploited, and face oppression, in societies organized around structural white supremacy it isn't possible to be racist against white people. For white people, mainstream society is their safe space, but as the dominant group in society they are left weirdly vulnerable and unable to ask questions about their own racialized identity. The basis of white people's structural advantage in white supremacist society today is the invisibility that whiteness affords, and perversely, this is a major inhibitor for white people who are seeking ways to live different, more human, more liberated lives. We are serious when we say white people need safe spaces to deradicalize, to be weaned away from toxic relations like racism and white supremacy, which dangle power and security at the price of their humanity.

KEY PRINCIPLE:

White people experience many forms of intersecting oppression, but they cannot experience racism because we live in a world structured by white supremacy.

HOW DO WE FIX PAST WRONGS WITHOUT CREATING NEW ONES?

It takes a lot of effort to try to fix a system when you are just a small part of it. A common discussion in SSFWQ arises from white people worrying about making mistakes that could harm nonwhite people. In an unfair society, it is natural to internalize and perpetuate this unfairness unless deliberately working not to.

It's easy to feel discouraged when the likelihood of "getting it wrong" is so high. Confronted with the gut-sinking feeling of doing it wrong, there is an understandable desire to shield yourself from embarrassment by doing nothing or seeking some relative protection by joining up with a larger group (the political party, the union, the church, the book club, etc.). But there is value in training yourself to welcome the accountability that comes from making a well-intentioned mistake, and this learning will help in both your individual and collective efforts to fight systemic injustices. By making a mistake in a good way — meaning you manage your feelings when someone criticizes you and then do a bit of homework to better understand the politics of race — you can learn most effectively and model what racial resilience looks like to those around you. It takes good preparation and a great deal of courage to be willing to be wrong on the way to making right.

Another important reason to embrace an ethic of making good mistakes: colonial capitalism works to ensure its longevity by keeping people exhausted and nervous about taking public stands on controversial issues, limiting their political imagination about what the world can look like. Tired workers who are offered festive cookies and a glass of wine every now and again by the boss are kept perpetually busy, scampering around looking for a weekend reprieve or a bottle instead of organizing across their many complex differences and building the world they deserve. Acting in good faith means you will make mistakes along the way, and committing to making good mistakes means that you will not only learn from those mistakes but model how to mature your thinking with experience. This can inspire others around you to do it too, and a society with members interested and willing to stand up for one another is the greatest threat to the status quo. Beware the liberal and conservative dictum that you need to have everything figured out before you try to change society. You don't, and you can't.

This broad theme of how to fix past wrongs without making new ones comes from many kinds of anxious questions white people have asked us. We notice the tendency is to think the past is history and to worry about how to change the *present* to build a better society for everyone without taking things away from some of the people who have things now. Many people have expressed concern about movements like Land Back because they fear the homes of white people might be seized by Indigenous people. Similarly, they panic about priority hiring of equity-deserving groups, thinking their sons will not get a fair shake. Some fear "cancel culture" is leading to a world in which a diversity of viewpoints is not valued, maybe even causing great harm to the country itself by challenging the narratives it is built upon. Even folks who are committed to positive social change struggle to find ways to explain to those close to them that taking an honest look at Canadian history involves challenging many of the assumptions that society takes for granted.

Reparations, Land Back

What reparations for colonialism and slavery might look like for white people is a very common concern for them. Most people start with the assumption that reparations for slavery or the return of stolen Indigenous territory means removing white people from their homes or from the public community in some way, a hyperbole that has been reported in the mainstream news. A better way of understanding reparations is to recognize that Canada is a mature society made up of more than just people originally from Europe — in fact, as Africana philosophy professor Chike Jeffers once explained, survivors of slavery are part of the Canadian public. State resources at our collective disposal can be used to address a grievous harm and theft of fundamental human rights that continues to impact society. In other words, reparations are not just white people giving their money to Indigenous or Black people; they involve the state prioritizing the health and well-being of those generationally impacted by colonialism and slavery.

Indigenous Nations and communities were, and continue to be, dispossessed of their land by Canadian settler-colonial capitalism. This takes the form of projects often seen as ecologically conscious and democratically determined, because settler-colonial institutions like elected legislatures and the professional bureaucracy evaluate proposals and authorize them. Indigenous people are obviously part of Canadian society, but unlike other people on this territory, they are *also* connected to their own Nations and communities, which have been directly harmed through the historical and ongoing deception and violence of Canadian state expansion. So when blockades or other actions where Indigenous people enact their sovereignty happen, Indigenous people are not causing a conflict with Canada. Britain, France, and later Canada caused the conflict by failing to honour the inherent equality of Indigenous sovereignties across the continent.[8] In the same way that no one would suggest that Canada could simply establish a development project in Florida without multi-jurisdiction permissions, so too should it be expected that Canada and Canadian corporations will not be able to extract resources in Mi'kmaw, Algonquin, or Wet'suwet'en territory without permission if sovereignty is respected.

While we hear concerns with alarming regularity that "Indigenous people want to take private property" back, we have never once encountered any Indigenous Nation, scholar, or activist who has communicated a desire to seize anyone's home. It simply is not part of the ask of Land Back, broadly conceived, which is mostly concerned with what is problematically called "Crown" land, or land that belongs to the state. How did the state come to "own" this land?

Perhaps little else captures the spectacular arrogance of empire better than the "waste land ordinances" applied by the British Empire in South Asia. Generally, the ordinances said any land not being used "productively" (read: for economic and commercial exploitation) was considered unused or "wasted" and thus became public property to be used for the benefit of the state. This justification for systematically stealing land from Indigenous Peoples and giving it to the state for redistribution to settlers was used all over the world. As Indigenous Peoples have gone to great lengths to explain, what lost white people perceived as "wasted" land was the very enactment and practice of complex and nuanced Indigenous worlds and culture.[9] Moreover, viewing land as a commodity fails to recognize that land means much more than "resources" to Indigenous Peoples whose languages and cultural traditions developed alongside *particular* lands for thousands of years.

Reparations, as Shashi Tharoor has eloquently explained, is not just about financial compensation but also the broader project of atonement for evil. Tharoor offered as an example of meaningful reparations for more than two centuries of colonial occupation and destruction that the British government could give India one pound every year for two hundred years.[10] The cost would be small — a mere 200 pounds — but it would serve the purpose of public atonement. Tharoor is an Indian politician and best-selling author, so atonement may be enough for him, but on the issue of reparations we stand firmly with African Nova Scotian community leaders like Lynn Jones and Robert Wright who have made serious cases for financial reparations to be paid by the state to survivors of the slave trade and colonialism. Again, this is not something individuals are giving to other individuals but something that

Canada (representing all people in the country) would contribute to address a problem that Canada has had a role in creating and sustaining.

Let's talk about one example of reparations. The first free modern state in the western hemisphere was not the United States (as much as Americans might think it was) but Haiti, where enslaved people overthrew their slave owners and multiple waves of European armies to create a society free from slavery in 1804.[11] France, Great Britain (and thus Canada too as part of the British Empire), and the United States forced the fledgling state to pay reparations to the white slave owners who had lost their "property." Please take a moment to let that sink in, if this is new information: enslaved people who won their freedom were made to pay because they were no longer owned by white people. Making self-emancipated people pay damages for the losses of their oppressors has had an intergenerational and rippling economic effect throughout the history of the modern world, and Haiti — now one of the poorest countries in the world — is offered the indignity of aid tied to Western development regimes instead of the reparations the country is entitled to. This example shows how the politics of fearing reparations to survivors of slavery and colonialism is old and steeped in both hypocrisy and white supremacy.

Lots of people have asked, "But where will the money come from?" This question is not asked when governments bail out large corporations like airlines and banks, so there's a double standard to be acknowledged here. State money is there; the political will to redirect that money is missing. One idea that has gained considerable traction across Canada is defunding police and redistributing those funds to social programs and services better suited to address structural and intergenerational racism. Despite the massive amounts of public money spent on policing (ten times more funding than employment and social services receive in the City of Toronto's budget, for example), there is no conclusive evidence to suggest that spending more money on policing decreases crime. Alternatively, examples show investing in addressing socioeconomic disparities and creating opportunities does decrease crime.[12] Evidence-based public policy research can find ways to redirect funds towards concrete investments in reparations and land back that could also diminish the need for bloated police budgets. We explore defunding more directly in Chapter 10.

More importantly, national conversations about land back and reparations need to be evolving, progressive discussions between the state (as the representative of Canada or one of its provinces or territories) and the different communities seeking reparations and land back. It ought not to be a conversation aimed at eliminating future land issues or "settling" the issue of slavery (which has barely started in Canadian society) because the point is precisely the opposite — to sustain ongoing public education about and accountability for these atrocities while creating avenues to repair their effects as identified by the communities living with their long-term consequences.

That said, in some instances white settlers have decided voluntarily to return land they inherited or bought when they realized it was stolen from Indigenous people. This direct form of reconciliation can be useful as well, but it's important not to overrepresent this (as the media does) as an act of charity, which then hides the violence of the theft as well as the inherent sovereignty of Indigenous Nations and communities to make decisions about land they have not ceded.

Learning to Eagerly Accept Criticism

White people have legitimate concerns about trying to work towards dismantling structural white supremacy while not inadvertently creating new problems. We conclude this chapter where we began — with a consideration of how to make mistakes in a good way.

The first step is to do a little research on your own; read what you can, and listen to audio and video recordings about the issues you're concerned about. A tremendous amount of material is available. If you have more specific questions, reaching out for some guidance from people who know more than you on a particular topic is usually not a bad plan. The key here is to listen actively to what racialized people are already saying and doing, and then answer calls for help and support. We have been to many rallies, for example, where community organizers have asked participants to make a special effort to organize white people to show up on the streets to demand justice for Black and Indigenous victims of state violence. Sometimes it is enough of a starting point to simply turn up and be counted, and the deep learning can proceed from there.

You should never assume to be able to speak on behalf of anyone. If someone you love says they want to "give a voice" to a marginalized community, remind them that people have voices and the better work is to make sure everyone in your lives is capable of hearing what is being said. Along the way you will end up making mistakes, big or small, and how you behave afterwards is of the utmost importance. Allow us to illustrate with another personal anecdote.

A little more than a decade ago, Ajay was participating in a poetry reading at a No One Is Illegal fundraiser, reading part of a poem alongside three women of colour (two of them Black, one of them South

Asian). One of the lines Ajay read included the slur "sand[n-word],"
which is used against people of Middle Eastern and South Asian
descent. After the performance he was confronted by an extremely
respectful and serious Black person, who thanked him for his contribu-
tions and proceeded to tell him that under no circumstances should he
use the n-word. In that moment, Ajay was defensive. He did not write
the poem, he was just performing it, the British had used the n-word
to describe Indians in the nineteenth century, and further he had been
targeted with the slur many times. Ajay *argued*, and in the process of
that argument he also misgendered the person who was trying to offer
a correction on a mistake of great importance. At the time Ajay had
little understanding of gender diversity and was genuinely confused
when bystanders told him the person's pronoun was "they."

In this moment Ajay failed miserably at making a mistake, because
rather than calmly listening and taking the time to understand a
constructive criticism, he first sought to prove that the person offering
the criticism was wrong by being defensive about his ancestry and
own experiences of racism. He failed to think about the immediate
intersectional kind of harm he was causing to gender-diverse Black
people in the room by instead focusing on empirical historical questions
grounded in the nineteenth century. The Black person offering the

* * *

Constructive criticism, *noun*
A respectful way of giving and receiving feedback motivated by a genuine desire to help
the receiver deepen their knowledge and understanding of an issue. Both the receiver and
offerer should be ready, calm, and interested for it to be successful.

criticism was being generous — they called him in with a desire to educate rather than calling him out — but Ajay's racial fragility and ego blocked him from understanding this as an act of solidarity, not an attack or attempt to cancel or deplatform him or the poet whose work he was reading. Amid this fragility and defensiveness, he was also unable to understand that he was misgendering the person offering the criticism, thus further aggravating the situation. To be clear, the mistake was how Ajay managed his emotional response and not necessarily what he said before he learned how it affected the person giving him feedback.

Upon reflection, Ajay has tried to apply two important lessons he learned from the experience. First, regardless of his views on the historical context of the n-word, the use of the n-word by a non-Black person induced genuine trauma for a Black listener. As it is within Ajay's power to simply not use the n-word, he is happy to avoid it to prevent harming others. This does not require agreeing about the nuances of the term; it requires respecting the humanity of those with differing points of view on a subject. Second, Ajay spent a long time seeking out education about 2SLGBTQ+ politics, which is far from his lived experience as a hetero and cis man. He feels shame and regret about how he reacted, but in turning the experience into a point of critical reflexivity and vehicle for public education he hopes to honour the spirit of the good criticism he received.

● ● ●

Cis, *noun / adjective*
A term indicating that a person's assigned sex at birth matches their gender identity. Often used as an opposite to "trans."

It is important to just listen when someone is offering constructive criticism. Depending on the person's capacity and what they have been experiencing in the moment, they may not be polite or put together. But part of your responsibility as an ethical person developing the chops to make mistakes in a good way is to accept the words as they come to you and to commit to thinking on the substance of the criticism as opposed to your immediate feelings about it. Your feelings in the moment will be predominantly triggered by your sense of fragility and defensiveness, which are very real feelings and also very unhelpful feelings that need to be managed. That said, no one should accept abusive behaviour masquerading as constructive criticism. When you are attacked for having a different point of view on an issue, it is perfectly fine to defend yourself and it is important to stand up to abusive behaviour. There are no firm rules about how to tell the difference between one and the other, but if you learn to keep your emotions in check when someone is disagreeing with you, then your racial fragility will no longer be an obstacle to determining when someone is trying to help you (as in the example above) and when they are trying to hurt you or silence you. Practice makes perfect!

— ⊕ ————————————————————————

KEY PRINCIPLE:

The process of building alternatives requires courage and humility to make good mistakes and draw meaningful lessons from those mistakes so the generosity of those who help you to learn is not squandered.

HOW DOES RACISM RELATE TO OTHER FORMS OF OPPRESSION?

Experience and observation confirm there are, unfortunately, a multitude of ways to degrade other groups of people. Whether along the lines of gender, race, sexuality, class, age, ability, belief, nationality, or more, people seem capable of imagining a dizzying array of ways to dehumanize others. The systematic and widespread diminishment of the dignity of other groups of people is what we refer to as oppression. When specific groups of people are identified as less than fully human, bad things happen. History is filled with nightmarish examples of what happens when groups of people are denied membership in our common humanity. But oppression is not natural or inevitable. No one is individually to blame for the state of the world, but by virtue of being born into it everyone is responsible for it. It also means people can do something about oppression and build a better, more liberated society along the way. The relationship between different kinds of oppression, including racism, is at the heart of this chapter.

A common narrative in many allegedly mature liberal democracies such as Canada and the United States goes like this: While there used to be real injustices, progress has been made on all of the big issues. Women have the right to vote, Indigenous people are not being forced to assimilate, Black people are no longer enslaved, and "diversity" and "inclusion" are watchwords everywhere from corporate boardrooms to public institutions. This tidy liberal myth imagines oppression as something frozen in time rather than a dynamic social relation belonging to its context. It suggests postracial societies have taken shape because formal segregation has ended, the United States elected a Black president, and plenty of diversity is represented in pop culture. Of course, none of this touches the entrenched and widening discrepancies in wealth across racial lines or the fact that racialized people remain disproportionately vulnerable to state-sanctioned imprisonment, violence, and death. This story is a convenient fiction in defence of the status quo and the ruling class at the heart of it. After all, if you don't see alternatives as viable, you are very unlikely to struggle towards them.

● ● ●

Oppression, *noun*
A collective social phenomenon involving the debasement of a group of people by another group that aims to maintain structured inequality, with tangible, lived, and material benefits for the oppressors and tangible, lived, and material costs for the oppressed.

Instead, "social justice snowflakes" are treated to an endless pillorying for supposedly screeching nonsensical demands that seek to take away what little the rest of us have by working hard and playing by the rules. The message is that these groups are playing identity politics, crying about oppression while fattening themselves at the trough of an overly tolerant mainstream. Instead of encouraging people to approach each other with empathy as a first step to building something better together, this story provokes them to turn against each another, as if they were dogs fighting over scraps fallen from their master's table. Solidarity and social justice are not zero-sum games; the more one group has does not mean there is less for everyone else, yet people are often encouraged to see alternatives to the status quo in precisely this way. While it's true the world has finite resources and so decisions must be made about how best to use them, it's a potent ruse to get everyone who is exploited and oppressed to fight each other rather than band together against those who exploit and oppress.

People are inundated with stories about a bewildering array of seemingly niche grievances. A sprawling, all-consuming media landscape is designed to superheat emotional responses and keep individuals clicking, not facilitate a nuanced and thoughtful conversation about the state of the world. Sensational and superficial stories about the issue or movement of the moment take the place of trying to achieve a real understanding of how society is organized and how power works. This frequently leaves people with the sense of *something* being deeply wrong — they're just not sure what it is or what to do about it. So how can you make sense of racism and its relation to other forms of oppression? One way to start is by grappling with two concepts: identity politics and intersectionality.

Who's Afraid of Identity Politics?

What is identity politics and why are so many people talking about it? For some, especially those who rarely find themselves up against society's cutting edges, identity politics represents the height of social justice warrior snowflake culture. In its most unflattering caricature, it is a shrill, denunciatory, and moralistic attempt to lay claim to victim status and leverage it to gain access to opportunities, resources, or social standing. But is this what identity politics actually is?

The term entered radical political discourse in North America in the 1970s by way of a group of radical, socialist, Black lesbian feminists calling themselves the Combahee River Collective (CRC). The group settled on the concept of identity politics to describe their political orientation and how it differed from other feminist politics. For the CRC, identity politics simply meant "that the most profound and potentially most radical politics come directly out of our own identity, as opposed to working to end somebody else's oppression."[13] Caught between white women's feminism and Black men's antiracism,

● ● ●

Identity politics, *noun*
A term coined in the 1970s by the Combahee River Collective, a group of Black, lesbian, radical feminists in the United States, out of a conviction that "the most profound and potentially most radical politics come directly out of our own identity, as opposed to working to end somebody else's oppression."

both of which neglected them, these women needed to carve out a space to focus on their own liberation. In its original configuration, identity politics was not about claiming some special pride of place for a given group; it was about understanding that oppression is always contextual and experiential.

Let's take a moment to think through the CRC's statement and what it means. There's nothing in the statement or the original concept of identity politics that asserts essential goodness or badness for any particular group. As the CRC insists, "To be recognized as human, levelly human, is enough." Nor does this framing revel in victimhood, denunciations, or moralism. Quite the opposite. For the CRC and the radical political legacy they bequeathed to us, identity politics is a concept that insists on understanding the lived, material reality of oppression as the necessary first step in the journey towards collective liberation.

Oppression is not about disagreements or even interpersonal abuse. It is an organized social relationship based on the debasement of a group of people by others to maintain structured inequality that accrues material benefits for the oppressors and material costs for the oppressed. For example, however someone might feel individually about abortion, it's pretty uncontroversial to note that women's bodies, sexuality, and reproductive function are legislated, monitored, and policed in a way that men's simply are not. It's possible to imagine making abortion illegal by surveilling, legislating, and policing men's bodies instead or in addition to everyone else's, but that is not the reality. Why not? Oppression can take any form *potentially* but not *in actuality*. That's because history matters.

As explored in Chapter 1, under conditions of structural white supremacy the only racism possible is racism directed against nonwhite people. Racism is not about bad feelings. It's not about having bad thoughts or negativity towards people individually. It's a structural power relationship between identified groups of humans. Racism is like a container of really awful, toxic relations. It can potentially take any form based on the power relations of its context. In our context, racism is bound up with white supremacy because of the historical trajectory of the last five hundred years.

Identity politics is not about certain groups of people being essentially and eternally heroes or villains, which we elaborate on in Chapter 7. It's about understanding how power works in specific contexts. This critical understanding is vital to not only diagnosing current social problems but also figuring out how humanity might live otherwise. That's not about performative, hypermoralistic grandstanding. That's necessary work in the struggle for all to live more liberated lives.

Intersecting Privileges and Oppressions

Right up there with "identity politics" and "critical race theory," the term "intersectionality" provokes ire, hatred, and contempt from the right because it is misunderstood as an affront to equality. Black

• • •

Intersectionality, *noun*
Coined by Kimberlé Crenshaw, this term refers to the overlapping nature of social identity categories, such as race, class, gender, sexuality, age, and ability, and how they work together to sustain structured social relations of privilege and oppression.

feminist scholar Kimberlé Crenshaw coined the term to talk about how different kinds of oppression and privilege exist for a person simultaneously.[14] For Crenshaw, making visible the rich complexity of Black women's positionality in the United States was vital. As a legal scholar, she used examples grounded in legal discrimination issues, such as a court decision to throw out a claim by Black women auto workers that they were unfairly laid off because of their race and gender. Because the auto plant in question employed Black men and white women, the court found the company did not discriminate based on race (due to the presence of Black men) or gender (due to the presence of white women). Crenshaw's response is simple but potent: Black women are both Black and women, and these attributes of their identity cannot be separated. Both aspects work together to create Black women's lived experiences, which differ from Black men's experiences and white women's experiences. All of these groups are treated differently and experience life differently from one another.

If this is true for Black women, it is true for everyone. Both of us are nonwhite men, and part of our experience includes various forms of discrimination against us because we are not white and do not hail exclusively from a white or European cultural context. It is worth noting that although some people may perceive us as Black (which has happened), our historical struggles as people of South Asian (and Latvian, in the case of Alex) descent mean that we don't experience the anti-Black racism or anti-Indigenous racism characterizing settler colonies with deep roots in the slave trade, such as Canada and the United States. Further, we have not suffered any discrimination as a result of being cis men born into a world sustained by patriarchy, or the systematic privileging of men. We were raised in working-class homes, and this is foundational to how we both came to understand the practical unfairness of life under capitalism well ahead of taking up the study of it later in life. Unlike our male privilege, our class privilege has changed over time because we now both have stable salaries and middle-class jobs. So while class is something that intersects our experiences as nonwhite men, it is changeable in ways that race is not.

We're talking about ourselves at length in this book, because we want to illustrate that everyone is privileged in some ways and disadvantaged in other ways, and those experiences are intricately tied to our contexts. Learning about patriarchy was a transformative experience for us that offered a way to see ourselves in an oppressive position simply because we were born as men in a patriarchal society. Society is not structured *only* by patriarchy; it is also simultaneously structured by many other things, some good, some bad, and some more difficult to define through a binary of good and bad. Men also suffer under patriarchy; toxic masculinity is a very real problem. But thinking through this point reminds us of the recurring theme in this book: do not confuse agents and structures when trying to understand how the world works. Patriarchy is one structure that permeates society and privileges people for no other reason than that they are men. But

• • •

Patriarchy, *noun*
Literally "rule of the father," it is a form of oppressive social organization in which men hold power, dominate roles of political or economic leadership, exert moral authority, and exercise disproportionate privilege and control of property.

white supremacy is another structure within society that privileges people who appear to be white, which excludes us. More than that, it categorizes us into a racial hierarchy that has no scientific validity yet endless social, political, and economic consequences.

To understand how different relations of oppression are interwoven it's useful to go back to the end of the 1800s in England and a man named Sir Francis Galton. He was a cousin of Charles Darwin's, and he ended up riffing off some of Darwin's ideas about evolution and misapplying them to people and society. His theories would become the basis for eugenics, a pseudoscientific belief system that falsely asserts that specific abilities are heritable and so possible to cultivate in or eliminate from society through the selective breeding of people. Eugenics has become the basis for extermination policies across a variety of colonial contexts but also domestically against "undesirable" populations — poor, disabled, racialized, and more. Galton's theories and eugenics essentially posit that some people's lives are unworthy; the Nazis referred to them as "useless eaters," and they were among the first targeted for extermination.[15]

The animating force behind this murderous junk science is the idea that selectively breeding and culling populations will better serve the interests of the ruling class and advance their attempts to take wealth, exercise power over territory, and outcompete other elites in other contexts. Keep in mind there's not a shred of reliable evidence for any of this. It is an attempt to justify relations of oppression and exploitation already in process. Five centuries ago at the birth of the modern age, when Western European powers were engaged in the interimperial competition for labour, land, and resources, this debate was not framed in genetic or hereditary terms but in terms of whether Indigenous people had souls or were born "natural slaves." If they had souls they could be brought to Christianity and depriving them of their liberty, territory, and resources was a violation of God's law. On the other hand, if they were "natural slaves," then they were not fully human and so colonizers could do anything to them that they pleased without committing a sin. Whether five centuries ago or today, dehumanization is critical to facilitating exploitation and exercising power over other people, territory, and resources. There is continuity and overlap in the racist thinking described here and the application of twentieth- and twenty-first-century public policy in Canada, whether it be the so-called Indian Residential Schools, medical experimentation on Inuit, or the systematic and multijurisdictional targeting of African Nova Scotians to displace, impoverish, and incarcerate.

Here's another current example. COVID-19 has sickened and killed millions of people around the world, profoundly disrupting life as usual. It has also provided a stark backdrop against which to explore the intersection of toxic social relations of oppression, bringing with it a vigorous upsurge in anti-Asian racism, harassment, and violence, particularly in North America. Despite the novel coronavirus's murky origins, many pundits, politicians, and other opinion makers quickly blamed its emergence not only on China as a state but also on Chinese people and their supposedly barbaric cultural practices, such as selling live animals for consumption at "wet markets." Right-wing politicians and pundits regularly referred to COVID-19 as the "kung flu" or the "Chinese virus," whipping up anti-Asian sentiment in a context where people were already afraid and anxious. As law enforcement agencies across Canada and the United States have reported, the result has been a dramatic spike in anti-Asian hate crimes, with some cities reporting 700 percent increases over previous years.

In one particularly horrific example of such violence, in March 2021 a twenty-one-year-old white man struggling with a sexual addiction he understood as betraying his fundamentalist Christianity murdered six Asian women working at two massage parlours in Atlanta, Georgia. When arrested by police, the killer explained his motivation was to assist others with similar addictions by removing what he perceived to be their source — Asian sex workers. Here is a grisly example of the intersection between forms of oppression including classism, misogyny, sexism, and racism. Police described the mass murderer, in peak white supremacist terms, as simply "having a bad day." Struggling with his sexual desires, religious fundamentalism, and likely a host of other issues as well, he expressed his angst by killing women who not only represented his object of desire but also did not count as fully human because of their gendered and racialized identity. They were targeted because they were sex workers, but it is not sex work that set them up for this. They were targets because of their existence at the intersection of multiple kinds of oppression coding certain people and their bodies as the property of white men. We would be remiss if we did not also mention the long-standing tradition of sexually objectifying and exoticizing nonwhite women for men — and particularly white men — to fantasize about, consume, and discard.

It's a characteristic of power relations in settler-colonial societies to silo different forms of structural violence and force people to choose between them. You can deal with sexism or racism but not both at the same time. If those in power can compel everyone else to play their game and choose between oppressions, they can better manage and prevent people from building horizontal solidarities to fight back against them. To get out of this trap necessitates talking about whiteness and structural white supremacy as a sinew that connects all these experiences of oppression. Real collective liberation begins with a willingness to do that work.

KEY PRINCIPLE:

Racism is one especially odious form of structural oppression that intersects with other forms of structural oppression, such as classism and misogyny. Race is not biologically real, but the implications of who counts as fully human, and the material consequences of that, certainly are.

HOW CAN I MAKE ANTIRACISM PART OF MY FAMILY LIFE?

Discussions about forms of structural violence such as racism, white supremacy, misogyny, or settler colonialism often ping-pong between the very abstract and the individually concrete. Stories tend to focus on big ideas and society-spanning forces or shrink this abstract vastness to the fishbowl of individual biography. Fascism is depicted as a monolithic force looming over and threatening to smite humanity, or it's reduced to Adolf Hitler's childhood and failed aspirations as a painter. What gets lost in looking only at these extremes? What about the relationships and contexts that make up the fabric of people's day-to-day lives? What do racism and antiracism have to do with kin relations and families, including those people are born into and those they choose?

Kin relations are the substance of human lives, not least because this is the level at which individuals sustain themselves on a daily basis. They take care of the old and the young, the sick and the infirm. They raise children and socialize them into the world. They make food, celebrate birthdays and holidays, argue about things important and trivial, tell stories about who they are and where they come from, and craft all kinds of other social meaning in the midst of this everyday living together.

These intimate spaces of family life are also where relations of oppression are reproduced or challenged. This is an area we frequently get questions about. Almost everyone can recount some (or perhaps many) awkward instances in their kin life where issues relating to oppression come up and cause no end of trouble. Perhaps it's a heated conversation around a dinner table. Perhaps it's in unpacking some of the attitudes and ideas they were raised with now that they have the time and distance to reflect. Perhaps it's in raising kids and confronting the harsh realities of white supremacy, misogyny, ableism, and any other form of structural violence that might shape their lives. Whatever the specific trigger, lots of folks have important and pressing questions about how to make antiracism a part of their family life.

Race Isn't Culture

One important thing to get out of the way at the outset: culture, the meaning-making work humans do, is not a synonym for race. Culture is the worldview and lifeway of people who consciously

● ● ●

Culture, *noun*
The shared conceptual framework and corresponding material practices belonging to a group of people who understand themselves as a distinct collective.

understand themselves as part of a larger social group. Put another way, it's the shared conceptual framework and corresponding material practices belonging to a group of people who understand themselves as a distinct collective. There's nothing about the melanin content of your skin in that definition, and there is no sense that this meaning-making work should correspond to the political borders drawn on maps.

It's very convenient, however, to conflate race and culture when it comes to justifications of oppression and exploitation. In this vernacular, white people are the inheritors of "Western culture," depicted frequently as the origin of philosophy, science, democracy, enlightenment, and progress. Other people are depicted as occupying a point on a line stretching from savagery and barbarism to civilization. So much is wrong with this that it's hard to know where to begin, but for our purposes here it's enough to point out how nonsensical the notion of civilizational cultures is. What is "Western culture" exactly? Is it Shakespeare and Greek philosophy? Is it American-dominated culture industries such as Hollywood? Does it include Latin America and the Caribbean? What about people of all different skin tones who were born and raised on the settler-occupied territories of North America and who have never known any other place to call home? To talk about all of this as one coherent culture is pretty silly.

Let's take a concrete example. Ajay and his partner are both of South Asian origin. To some it might seem they come from the same culture; after all, they're both brown-skinned and they eat similar foods. But Ajay was raised as a Hindu, and his partner was raised as a Muslim. On this point alone there's plenty of room for difference and divergence — especially given the long history of extreme violence between Hindu and Muslim communities on the Indian subcontinent and elsewhere — never mind their wider family histories or the routes by which their families came to Canada.

It's important to disabuse yourself of the notion that that race and culture are identical. What people have been socialized to understand as "race" is not at all the same as the meaning-making work of culture.

"Mixed" Families

People don't transmit identities, values, or histories through their genetics — that comes from the intergenerational care work they do in their kin relations. Whether conscious of this or not, they are constantly making choices about what's important to them, what they want to pass on to those who come after, what they wish they could leave behind, and what makes them who they are. Humans do this in every intimate relationship they have, but it's often much more clearly visible for those who come from different cultural or racialized backgrounds. In SSFWQ we often get questions from folks who are worried about losing their culture because they are in a relationship with someone from another cultural group. The stakes increase when kids come into the picture. Does this mean so-called mixed-race or intercultural relationships are more fraught with difficulties than homogeneous ones? In today's world, the answer certainly seems to be yes, but that's only because of the way race has been weaponized in the service of oppression and exploitation.

Let's explore this through another example close to home. Alex identifies as an "ambiguously racialized person." His father, from

Burma, was quite dark-skinned, and came to Canada by a circuitous route in his early adulthood. Alex's mother was born in Latvia, one of the Baltic states near Russia, and came to Canada in her teenage years, also by a circuitous route. Both were escaping insecurity and violence, not migrating by choice. They met in Toronto and ended up getting married and having a couple of kids. Because they came from very different backgrounds, they decided that Alex and his sister would be raised to fit into Canadian society as (mostly) white-passing people. As a consequence of being raised in what Alex describes as a quintessentially multicultural Canadian fashion, where diversity is celebrated superficially and only so long as it does not challenge or interfere with white supremacy, he is eternally disappointing people who are curious about his last name and family history — he doesn't know much, because his parents simply didn't want to talk about most of it. This is to say nothing of the parade of much more conflictual moments where he and his sister were told they were exotic interlopers rather than authentic (white) Canadians. It's deeply unsettling to be raised to fit into a white-dominated society, to learn to navigate the world according to its cultural codes, only to be confronted with still not quite fitting. Being raised to identify with the dominant cultural coordinates of a white supremacist, settler-colonial society did not give Alex or his sister full membership in a white-dominated society that sees them as not quite white.

Every society exerts a cultural gravitational pull on its members, which is why society is more than just the sum of all our individual lives and actions. This is no more or less true for children in mixed-heritage households, but it can present unique challenges for them. Those who can pass as white may feel pressure to not identify too openly with their racialized heritage. The desire to fit in, to belong, to feel at home, to not be too different or different in the wrong way, to not be identified as an "other," is powerful at any time. It is especially so in a world shaped by vast and growing inequality, endless war, militarized borders, and predatory capitalist maldevelopment.

Ultimately, every person needs to find their own way in the world, a task made much easier with the care, understanding, and support of kin. Though it is understandably important for elders to see their cultural practices, identities, stories, and values carried forward, youth are not merely vehicles for their legacies. Caregivers need to acknowledge the complicated feelings of ambiguously racialized youth in a structurally white supremacist society.

The resting face of Canadian society is white supremacist. We mean this empirically, not moralistically. As a fragment of Western European empire-building founded on the displacement, dispossession, and genocide of Indigenous Peoples, Canada is a white supremacist state. Settler-colonial institutions based on Western European ones (parliaments, courts, schools, police, etc.) set the baseline for authority and legitimacy. Settler-colonial legal systems assert their right to adjudicate claims made against the settler-colonial state by Indigenous Peoples whose existence on these territories vastly predates that state. The same state simultaneously asserts the right to adjudicate what other newcomers are allowed into these territories, discriminating against the racialized and the poor in every iteration of its immigration system. Canadian society is not some kind of neutral space where everyone is free to be who they are; it's a product of the power dynamics that brought it into being. Canadians cannot escape this legacy without facing up to it.

One consequence of supremacist forms of thinking is the false notion that people experience the world in essentially the same way. This is nonsense, but it provides a convenient explanation for why the world is the way it is that does not challenge or question established power relations. In any intimate relationship, but perhaps especially in interracialized ones, it's important to develop the comfort and confidence necessary to talk frankly with your partner about issues you experience differently because of how you are positioned in the world, and then to talk to your children about what it means to be seen as racially ambiguous. Be honest with yourself about what is important to you in terms of what values, identities, histories, and practices you want to carry forward in a relationship.

Many of those who live in places far away from where their ancestors did — as part of what is known as the diaspora — are frequently plagued by the feeling of not quite fitting in anywhere. They're neither authentic products of their cultural roots nor easily at home in the societies they live in. But the diasporic condition is legitimate, experienced by many people, and no less authentic than

● ● ●

Diaspora, *noun*
A dispersed population of people who share a common place of origin. For example, a sizeable Trinidadian diaspora lives in the Greater Toronto Area.

the experiences of those who remain physically connected to their ancestral homelands. For example, Ajay is a doubly diasporic member of the South Asian community via the Caribbean and Canada. Is he Indian? Caribbean? Canadian? Against what yardstick should the authenticity of his life experience be measured? Identity is more complicated than that, and coming to terms with the fluidity and complexity of your identities and experiences should not preclude you having access to your ancestors.

Guess Who's Coming to Dinner?

If there's one thing close to a universal truth, it's that family drama is real. Marriage is typically seen as the culmination of monogamous, pair-based, romantic love, but it's much more than two people being joined in ceremony. Two different families are coming together too. IN-LAWS. Dun, dun, duuun.... The ensuing joy, friction, and strife are a major human preoccupation, and that's just judging by Hollywood comedies. We get lots of questions about how to handle difficult conversations about social justice in extended family settings. Many people have had the experience of being involved in an explosive political discussion around the dinner table or at some family event. Many folks, understandably, want a set of strategies for intervening more successfully in these minefields.

If you're in a long-term relationship, you are building relationships not just with your partner but with their family as well. This is not a sprint, it's a marathon, and prioritizing what you see as the key long-term goals to achieve in that context is worthwhile. Also of importance is personally reflecting on the source of your irritation or frustration.

If you're running into ways of relating that just don't map onto what you know from your own experience, wading into conflict with people you're trying to build long-term relationships with is likely not the best course of action. You cannot possibly fight every battle or see everything that bothers you as a reason for another argument. Often, arguing about something is the least effective way of making change on the subject. For example, in Ajay's extended family context he noticed a highly gendered division of household work. Rather than calling it out and making a spectacle of the issue, he just started cleaning up and doing the dishes after family dinners. At first this was actually fairly awkward for him, because men were not typically expected to do this work, and so it was the object of some ridicule and joking. Rather than give in, Ajay just kept doing it and, in so doing, normalized it. Eventually, at the very least, it was silly to make fun of doing it. No revolutionary changes occurred, and Ajay's housework didn't bring the patriarchy tumbling down, but he tangibly contributed to household labour and simply set a different kind of example. This is an example of an intervention in a gendered division of labour that did not take the form of conflict to make a point.

At the same time, the understandable desire to avoid conflict should not be an excuse to give a pass to all kinds of oppressive behaviour. Sometimes conflict is necessary and productive, an important part of healthy relationships. At the end of the day, no one should feel they must surrender their dignity for the sake of keeping the peace — that is precisely how everyday forms of oppression sustain their presence. Based on our experiences and the accounts of many others, people let things slide plenty of times — not because these issues don't deserve to be called out but because people become habituated to them. They learn to stay silent in the face of all kinds of insults and barbs because they don't want to be seen as the ones upsetting the family equilibrium. But is that what they're doing? Why does the fault not lie with the person or people imposing their dehumanizing, degrading, and oppressive behaviour on others? Justice, fairness, collective liberation, and even simply decent, fair-minded coexistence cannot be advanced by expecting one person or group to absorb endless blows.

If you are experiencing significant conflict in your extended family life and your humanity is being trod upon by people who are supposed to be your kin or might be kin one day, then ignoring it really isn't a solution. Begin a conversation with your partner and see where they're at. It can be as basic as saying something like, "Your family member said this thing to me. I found it really hurtful [and racist, sexist, whatever it might have been]. Is this something that usually happens?" Getting a read on that is very useful to figure out how to move forward. If you're not getting support from your partner on issues like this, then it's probably time to have a frank conversation with them about why that is. In a white-dominated society such as Canada, racialized people find themselves in these contexts frequently, and the expectation that they're going to be polite and keep the peace is its own form of violence. It's much less common to experience a physical confrontation than it is to be dehumanized in a million subtle ways having to do with manners, convention, the words people use to describe ethnic backgrounds, and more. Just because these are not physical forms of violence does not mean they should be things people have to endure.

The way to ultimately get out of this mess is by building and maintaining clear conflict resolution strategies and the capacity to have difficult and complex conversations so people can describe what is making them mad and what is at the root of their conflicts. When people become caregivers, the pressures of daily life can lead to anger and upset about things that they feel legitimately and deeply aggrieved about. Sometimes when they have a moment to consider the issue in a soberer light, they realize their reaction was provoked by exhaustion and frustration. The daily work of getting by under white supremacist, heteronormative, settler-colonial capitalism is hard and produces a lot of emotional weight. This is true even for people who think they are benefitting from these relations, who appear to be at or nearer to the top of the pile. Each person is constantly dealing with existential weight that structures their conflicts and the ways they deal with it.

Raising Antiracist White Kids in a White Supremacist Society
One of the main challenges faced by caregivers trying to raise kids to be antiracist in this society is, well, white supremacy is all around them. Like fish in water, people are surrounded by white supremacy, which can make it hard to see. One of the most important things parents of white children can do is to help their children see how white supremacy operates on an everyday level. Part of what makes white supremacy so powerful is it fades into the background of society-as-usual: it's just society moving along, it's just human nature, it's the way things have always been. People are socialized from a

very young age to accept the world as it is, including all the forms of oppression and exploitation that structure it.

To debunk this toxic common sense, it's necessary to help kids see the cleavages in society, the structural violence that makes some people's lives so much more difficult. Understandably, many parents and caregivers want to protect kids from these harsh realities but it's also vital to recognize that some kids never have the opportunity to be protected like this; their realities are already shaped by that violence. Parents and caregivers also need to respect the intellectual and emotional abilities of children. Lying to them about the cutting edges of society won't save them or anyone else.

This doesn't mean you have to indoctrinate them with revolutionary theory (at least not right away!). In fact, it points towards the utility of more fundamental interventions. For example, the police are often heralded as heroes in popular media, so a useful starting point is to commit to not celebrating police as an institution with your kids. This does not mean you have to raise your kids to hate the police or other forms of authority in society, but if you're dedicated to raising antiracists you need to encourage the children in your life to be critical of dominant social structures, relations, and institutions. The police protect certain aspects of society, not everybody equally, and all the data in the world is available to show that (more about this in Chapter 10). The same could be said of a host of other authoritarian, violent, oppressive, and exploitative relationships that people are socialized to accept and even venerate as they grow up.

Just as it is possible to be a man who is pro-feminist, a straight person who is queer-positive, or an anticapitalist living in a capitalist society, a white person can be antiracist. White skin does not fate you to be a racist or a white supremacist. None of the ethical positions you come to in the world spring from a pregiven, essential identity. They are positions you come to occupy through conviction, and people change the world by deciding what those convictions are going to be. White kids are no more destined to be racist than anybody else. What matters is how you bring them into contact with the reality and experiences of structural violence in the world. Both of us are parents, and one of the things we have learned in the course of this experience is it's better to have these conversations in less ideological, abstract ways in favour of more everyday, commonsense ones that engage the things kiddos are concerned with and talking about. It really comes down to teaching kids about the collective humanity they are a part of and share in.

KEY PRINCIPLE:

Bringing antiracism into family life is essential and can be done through role modelling, building stronger mechanisms of communication between loved ones, and preparing kids to engage the world as it is.

HOW CAN I TALK ABOUT SOCIAL JUSTICE WITHOUT TURNING PEOPLE OFF?

There's a special moment when the eyes of the person you are talking to glaze over and they start thinking about what to eat for dinner. It usually happens by the time you're a few minutes into making your point, and it signals the very instant you have failed to get through to someone, even if they give a polite nod. By the second or third time you say something like "structural racism" or "settler-colonial crisis of epic proportions," the person is already thinking about dessert.

Progressives have a hard time talking to people who do not already share their views. For people on the mainstream right or centre of the political spectrum, this does not pose as much of a problem because their views are already considered to be "normal" within society, meaning they can say things like, "Well, human nature is about looking out for numero uno," or "I give to charity, so I'm a good person," and no one questions these views. To hold progressive views — middle-of-the-road ones or radical ones — puts you at a disadvantage, because the generally accepted starting assumptions about things like human nature or what society is and ought to be are deeply steeped in beliefs that normalize capitalism and "traditional" values.

Before a progressive can even begin making a point, they first have to chisel away at deeply rooted beliefs about human nature (e.g., there are only men and women; if people look out for themselves, the market can sort things out) and the "real world" (e.g., colonial wars and domination were unfortunate but inevitable; countries have always existed) that most people assume have always been true. Only if you first accomplish the Herculean task of getting someone to reconsider the seeming naturalness and inevitability of the status quo can you even begin to think about how to discuss remaking society in a more equitable way. Unfortunately, by this point, most people's attention spans have been spent and they might even think you're a pompous asshole for challenging their right to hold an opinion regardless of whether it is based on evidence. You end up feeling exhausted and the person you're talking to either doesn't understand your point or feels condescended to and becomes hostile to your ideas. It's really hard to talk about social justice with people who have privileges they do not believe exist.

It's not a one-sided problem; progressives must accept blame for this quagmire as well. Something is not correct simply because it's progressive. Towards what, for example, is society progressing? The truth is you cannot know the answer to that if you care about grassroots democracy and equity, because discovering it is an essential part of working together to build a better society. But to the progressives reading this book, take a minute to think about what that sounds like to someone who does not already agree with you.

> DUDE: Supposing "the system" could ever change, what's your idea?

> YOU: We need to dismantle capitalism and build something better.

> DUDE: What's better?

> YOU: Something that recognizes unpaid labour and the wage gap, treats housing as a human right, recognizes treaty rights, and refuses to be complacent with heteropatriarchal family structures!

> DUDE: Gotcha. (I'm totally gonna eat a burrito when I get off this bus.)

The dude archetype above may have lots of reasons to agree with you about all of these things, but they need to learn about it differently. We discuss some strategies in this chapter. Another archetype might be the middle-aged working-class conservative who has struggled most of her life to make ends meet (just like a working-class progressive in many ways) and whose hard-won personal security seems threatened by the notion of building a new society. There's good logic to this apprehension: if you've been harshly treated by the rules of society but still managed to make it, the thought of changing the rules of the game could be terrifying because it would, in principle, bring you back to square one. Fear of the unknown is a major inhibitor to communicating progressive politics to people who have lived experiences of oppression but have found some relative security in their life. Dogmatic beliefs grounded in too little evidence are not only the province of the right. Too often those on the left mirror similar belief-driven commitments to whatever it is they think, and as a result make the mistake of assuming that people who think otherwise do so because they are ignorant or uneducated. Aside from providing raw fodder for the rise of right-wing populism all over the world, this situation also gives rise to the prototypical self-righteous leftist. Whether you're the vegan who comes for breakfast and scowls at the lack of macadamia nut milk, the bearded Marxist who just needs everyone to focus on the elucidation of surplus value and profit in volume 3 of *Kapital*, or the dedicated anarchist who won't be co-opted by the insult of a ballot box, people can suffer from communication problems that block them from finding common ground with the people they care about and those they don't agree with.

This chapter is devoted to finding ways to talk about social justice issues without triggering that special moment when the person you're speaking with checks out. We make light of the above motifs of obnoxious leftists because we have inhabited them in some shape or form over the course of our lives, but we need to acknowledge that the pressing issues generating the most pushback these days are not light-hearted ones. They are life-and-death ones. Indigenous land defence projects, the movement for Black lives, struggles to house folks caught in the maelstrom of speculative real-estate bubbles and unregulated rental housing, and the built-in structural racism of policing are not light topics. An additional difficulty is when people on any side of the political spectrum have internalized an "it is what it is" outlook. When people say this, it feels like they have either given up on imagining a more compassionate and equitable world or never believed such a world was worth struggling for in the first place. Deciding when and how to engage, with a clear understanding of your audience, is essential for avoiding burning out while chiselling away at the armour of baseless and often nationalist assumptions of those around you.

Social Justice Jargon

There's a time and place for specialized forms of language. Specialized language allows people who are similarly trained to use terms to "stand in" for lots of learning so conversations can advance more quickly. For example, if we say "structural white supremacy" to one another, we know we are talking about how society has normalized the worldview that white people, culture, and ideas are more advanced than others. We are *not* talking about an individual white supremacist and what they might have done. To talk about white supremacy as a structure means recognizing that racist violence can occur even without the involvement of any white people. For example, an Asian lawyer could represent the federal government and argue that Indigenous kids should not be funded at the same level as non-Indigenous kids.

In contrast, the overwhelming majority of times we use "structural white supremacy" around people who are not familiar with the concept, they assume we're suggesting all white people are bad or society is run by neo-Nazis. When you encounter specialized language and don't know what it means, or worse, if the language isn't being used accurately, it can be misunderstood like structural white supremacy or just sound like noise — think Charlie Brown's teacher. One of the quickest ways to dismiss a critical argument is to declare it's full of jargon. This allows the person levelling the accusation of jargon to avoid saying, "I don't know what that term means. Can you please explain it?" Specialized language may make the user feel intelligent, but it's counterproductive in a situation like this.

A winning strategy to avoid repeating jargon is to be specific and illustrative. Rather than saying "Black people experience structural racism" to someone who is new to thinking about race in terms that are bigger than the individual, try saying something like this instead:

> Black people are six times more likely to be stopped by the police in Halifax than white people are. It's not just a couple of racist cops doing this. It's a problem across the police force, as shown by the large amounts of data collected on it. And this issue extends across all parts of society. The way Black children are followed around by security and retail workers while in commercial spaces or the way brown people are treated with extra scrutiny at border crossings illustrate how race is treated like a weapon in the interest of public safety.

That example requires that you have done a little bit of digging to have some useful facts at the ready to support your argument. But you probably don't plan ahead for the moment when people assert harmful assumptions about marginalized people in front of you (which occurs especially if you're white because of the unspoken assumption of white solidarity). This particular information about the city of Halifax and the operation of structural anti-Black racism comes from the Wortley

Report,[16] published a few years ago and widely commented on in the media. But it also reflects what African Nova Scotians have been saying for decades. One way of learning could be to keep up with the news, so you know a little bit about what's going on in your society. Another way is to listen to people with special expertise in racism, like those who have lived it their whole lives.

How else can you speak plainly about structural white supremacy in Canadian institutions? History and comparison are always useful allies in this endeavour. Look at the historical role the RCMP has played in "clearing" the West for settler colonialism, the blunt arms of state violence used against Indigenous people all the way through. Or for more contemporary examples, consider the police violence and crackdown against Indigenous land and water defenders in Mi'kmaw, Mohawk, and Wet'suwet'en territories. Contrast that to the police response to the white nationalists at the core of the so-called Freedom Convoy of 2022, who were treated with gentle consideration over a three-week period and gradually coaxed into custody during their illegal blockades and occupation of the city of Ottawa. These predominantly white protestors, having much in common with the predominantly

• • •

White solidarity, *noun*
The unspoken agreement that ideas, cultures, and norms originating in European culture are universally "normal" and all others deviate from this norm. In practice this works to cultivate white fragility by discouraging and derailing conversations that make white people feel uncomfortable about racial politics. Historically, white solidarity has been used to ensure class-based solidarities across racial groups are not sustained by offering small advantages to white workers.

white police force and state, were not seen as threats. This is part of how white solidarity is assumed and enacted. The convoy's white truckers (many of whom were not actually truckers) benefit from but are unaware of how structural white supremacy creates opportunities for white people that nonwhite people do not have.

Knowing Who Your Real Audience Is

Most people don't respond well to conflict, big or small, however. If someone is trying to pick a fight with you over an issue, that is often all the evidence you need that you are not going to be changing that person's mind in a conversation. Especially if this is happening in a public space (dinner table, social media, group chat), it is crucial to remember that you are actually speaking to the silent listeners as much as the person you are fighting with. As a result, maintaining your composure and modelling how to respond to accusations and assumptions with thoughtful information can go a long way towards getting your ideas across to people you didn't even know were listening. This is the case in virtual platforms but also true of intergenerational family and social moments as well. Your queer nibling may appreciate your efforts at making space for dissent even if they have not come out to you or anyone else. It's also good to remember that when you're being yelled at by someone belligerently trying to force their views onto you, you have most likely won the argument by virtue of keeping your cool. Conversely, if you find yourself yelling at someone, you might silence them in the moment, but you have likely lost a great deal of empathy from the silent observing majority. These aren't hard and fast rules, as everything depends on context. For example, there are stereotypes grounded in racism and patriarchy, like the "angry Black woman," that discourage Black women from participating in debates at all; some people are expected to "keep cool" more than others, with more significant consequences for not doing so. So when you're part of the silent listening minority, keep in mind that you can't dismiss what someone is saying because they are angry. Some people genuinely have a lot more to be angry about based on their lived experience and daily aggravations.

Keeping your cool can be difficult when someone is questioning the inherent humanity and dignity of an entire group of people, as often happens within closed social groups. Granny's offence at an image of a Black Jesus, for example, might enrage you, especially since the historical Jesus of Nazareth was a Palestinian Arab and most certainly not a white guy with wavy blond locks like supermodel Hansel from the Zoolander movies. But you freaking out at Granny's racism won't win her support or the support of your family WhatsApp group. It certainly isn't going to make life any better for Black Christians. So consider digging in for the long haul instead. Your diligent and ongoing work within your community and family is more valuable to people from racially marginalized groups than your principled outrage is. In fact, your outrage might be serving your desire to be seen as a good person.

Principled outrage and deplatforming is necessary at times, especially in public. Chapter 6 explores this concept through a discussion of cancel culture, so we won't belabour the point here. If the person you find yourself speaking with is a woman in a MAGA (Make America Great Again) or Canada First ball cap trying to block access to an abortion clinic, it's time to escalate your game and clear them out of the way. But if instead you find yourself talking to a Canada First or MAGA supporter who happens to be a person you know and have positive feelings for, you need a different strategy altogether. Try to let them do the talking and ask them to explain why they think the things they think. Listen carefully and hard; you are gathering useful information in this conversation. Often there are materially based root causes behind people's positions — for example, fear of losing their jobs. It is easier for them to blame something like immigration for this, in part because organized rightwing politicians encourage this kind of conclusion. Also, the idea that a person may be oppressed by the structure of capitalism is much harder to understand than "Samira from Somalia took my job." Take it easy; these are complex issues. *This* conversation may not be the one where you get through to the person — when it comes to our loved ones, the conversation is long term.

But let's face it, not every white conservative is just being bamboozled by the far right. Many, perhaps even most, genuinely believe what they believe and have more power in our society than racialized people do. This is the very meaning of being "marginalized" within society. Ajay, on more than one occasion and in more than one professional context, has been confronted by bosses telling him wildly racist and inaccurate information. Speaking up in a work environment requires a good deal of tact, and it comes at considerable risk. Ajay was fired from at least one job for speaking up, and he sat in hot water at a number of others for similar reasons. At the time he had fewer personal responsibilities and could accept the consequences. But if you can't, you need to think strategically about how these moments can provide educational fodder for other workers witnessing these interactions, outside of the watchful eyes of your employers.

Conspiracies, Incels, and the Far Right

Evidence-based arguments do not work with people who fall victim to conspiratorial thinking, because conspiracy theories are defined by their ability to aggressively discredit evidence and incorporate that into the conspiracy itself. QAnon's position that US president Donald Trump was leading the charge against the "deep state" to expose the international pedophilia ring of the Clintons and others was not dampened by the electoral defeat of Trump in 2020, because the story can shift to explain "no no no, this is the next step to the great plan, and now we have to do X or Y."

The best strategy in trying to reach people who believe in conspiracy theories is to understand their root anxieties and the architecture of why they might think what they do. A common conspiracy as we type these words is that MRNA vaccines have microchips inserted by Bill Gates for the purpose of controlling you, or possibly sterilizing you, or something to that effect. The source of their fear may be twofold: technology is changing at a pace they have difficulty following, and they feel scared or anxious about life in the pandemic. A conspiracy theory, especially one popularized on social media, offers a sense of security in the powerlessness of the moment. Rather than calling them a dope, walk or sit with them and ask, "What's happening in the world right now that worries you?" There are logical limits here of course, because if at the end of the day your Aunty really thinks Jewish people are running the world, they may be an irredeemable antisemite and the best thing might be to make sure they are not able to act on these opinions.

Another useful strategy, especially if the person is not usually prone to conspiratorial or racist thinking, is to empathetically try to educate them about media literacy. You might be surprised at how many people don't really understand the basics on this one, and with good reason. In the lifespan of a seventy-year-old person today, they would have done drills to hide under their desks in case of nuclear war, seen humans land on the moon, started work with typewriters, maybe had their first home computer in the late 1990s and needed a hand crank to make it work, and seen the collapse of daily newspapers. If you have lived through such enormous technological change, it is not intuitively obvious that clicking four or five times within a single article to continue reading means it's junk. Remember, people are sitting alone in their bedrooms doomscrolling. Especially if the person is an older adult, they are seeing the state saying — and society broadly agreeing — that their preventable death is not worth the inconvenience of wearing a mask. People are lonely, abandoned by the state, and discarded by market capitalism. The solace of a community of people who think there's something especially evil afoot makes sense. If alienation or loneliness might be a contributing aspect to a person's conspiratorial musings, spending quality time with them can probably be effective and maybe even mutually beneficial.

Some of this thinking may be applicable if you think there are men in your life who identify with or are at risk of becoming members of incel,

* * *

Incel, *noun*
This term, meaning "involuntary celibate," was originally coined by a woman but has since been adopted by men (of many racial backgrounds) and used to describe an online and transnational community that peddles misogyny based on a belief that women are denying them sex.

or "involuntary celibate," communities. Incels think women owe men sex and that denying sex to men humiliates them. Not all men who buy into this are white; in fact, much of the new research on this kind of thinking and association suggests men with a range of racial backgrounds participate while internalizing structural white supremacist and misogynist worldviews.[17] Incels, as an online community of men, tend to encourage one another to commit acts of lone-wolf terrorism targeting women, and there have been recent incidents of this in Canada, the United States, and the United Kingdom. De-escalation strategies and explorations of root causes of anxiety may help to steer someone thinking along the incel trajectory in another way. Because incels tend to be younger people, the technological factor may be less of a problem than the ambient misogyny, patriarchy, and racism that permeates much of popular culture. It's important to keep these people from hurting others, and themselves, as this online community also tends to promote self-harm and suicide.

KEY PRINCIPLE:

When involved in an argument or disagreement, look for the root causes and underlying anxieties leading a person to hold discriminatory views. Empathy and care can be more effective than condescension and disbelief, especially in terms of modelling better behaviour for the witnessing silent majority.

WHAT'S THE DIFFERENCE BETWEEN CULTURAL APPRECIATION AND CULTURAL APPROPRIATION?

Conversations about cultural appropriation have become increasingly common in recent years. Broadly speaking, cultural appropriation is the unjust use and abuse of cultural practices by someone from outside that cultural group. This seems straightforward, but, as usual, things get sticky when moving from the abstract to the concrete. Dressing up like an "Indian princess" or in blackface for Halloween is an obvious and insulting example of appropriation. But what about owning Indigenous art, doing yoga, salsa dancing, or enjoying food from different parts of the world? What is the line between respect-fully appreciating someone else's culture and grossly appropriating it? Does intent matter or is it only the outcome that counts? The aim of this chapter is to untangle these knots and provide some useful guide-posts about respectfully and responsibly exploring the world we share.

It's Not about Your Inner Truth

As with racism, it's vital to keep in mind that appropriation cannot be reduced to a person's intentions. If you want to appreciate and show love for a specific culture, then you really have to understand its history and its context. You have to do a little bit of homework. If you encounter something inspiring from another cultural context, learn about what it means to the people who created it. Based on that, explore whether it's appropriate for you to embrace in your own life, or whether it's something that doesn't belong to you.

Many respectful forms of cultural borrowing, learning, and exchange exist. Humans have always crossed boundaries, met one another, and shared food, tools, clothing, ideas, and almost anything else you can imagine. Culture is something people make together, something always growing and changing. It is not just "intellectual property," to speak in the acquisitive language of capitalism. At the same time, some forms of cultural expression — clothing, language,

* * *

Cultural appropriation, *noun*
The use and abuse of a group's cultural practices by someone from outside that group.

social relationships, cosmologies, art, ritual, and more — belong to their context and can't just be picked up and dropped into someone else's life without causing problems.

It's not uncommon for people to retreat to a defence of their own "inner truth" if pushed on the question of whether something they're engaged in is culturally appropriative. A capitalist society makes it seem like other groups' cultural practices and belief systems are a big buffet laid out for you to consume, for the right price, of course. This is also an effect of liberal multiculturalism, which celebrates superficial differences between peoples while negating differences that are truly challenging. People are encouraged to eat food, wear fashion, and dabble in spiritual, artistic, and wellness practices from a globalized marketplace of opportunity. But it's important to understand what is being offered and how, because at the same time people are told that Islam is incompatible with liberal values like democracy and freedom of speech, that the West is in a "clash of civilizations" with those who "hate our freedoms," and that some people — depending on their cultural values and the melanin content in their skin — are unfit to rule themselves.

The trouble with treating cultural diversity as a marketplace or an existential threat is it prevents sincere attempts to come to mutual understandings and negotiate coexistence across difference. Rather than figuring out how and on what terms everyone in society can live together, people are encouraged to see society as split between the mainstream and minority groups. Basically, the mainstream gets to set limits for what it's willing to tolerate, and minorities get to figure out how to fit into that structure. That's the crux of official Canadian multiculturalism. Liberal democratic societies including Canada and the United States are often described as tolerant, which is really shorthand for white-dominated society being enlightened, civilized, and decent. From this perspective, putting up with other people's weirdness is a mark of inherent goodness. Of course, the boundaries of tolerance are always set by the dominant group, which retains the right to revoke this tolerance. This is not respectful coexistence. At best it's condescension; at worst it's a thinly veiled reminder that belonging rests on conformity. So it's okay to be titillated by Egyptian belly dancing but decry the practice of veiling. You can wax poetic about Indigenous Peoples' relationship to the natural world but dismiss their aspirations for cultural resurgence and political self-determination. You can celebrate Black athletic and artistic achievements while openly wondering why it is that Black countries cannot seem to develop like the Global North. It's worth taking a hard look at why so many feel entitled to sample whatever they like from other cultural groups and contexts while denying the full humanity of the people from those groups and contexts.

Drawing the Line

Some things are pretty simple. Dressing up as somebody else's culture for fun on Halloween is a racist thing to do and you should avoid doing it. Full stop. Racist mascots in sports are another example of low-hanging fruit. Let's be clear: there is no good-faith defence of not only using someone else's cultural identity for your sports team's mascot but also using a racist caricature of it. If the script were flipped, and sports team and mascot names included derogatory terms for white people like "cracker," "whitey," or "redneck," many white people would be very offended and rightly call it out. So why even waste a breath defending the usage of "redskins," "Eskimos," and "chiefs"? Other people's lifeways are not your playground.

Does that mean white people shouldn't do yoga? No, it means approaching that practice by learning something about its roots and coming to appreciate the cultures that gave birth to it. For example, Alex loves martial arts and trains in Muay Thai kickboxing as well as Japanese and Brazilian jiu jitsu. Alex is not Thai, Japanese, or Brazilian, but he doesn't see studying martial arts not innovated by his ancestors as a form of cultural appropriation. He respects the practices and their roots by learning about their origins and the cultural and historical contexts from which they came. Brazilian jiu jitsu is one of the world's most popular martial arts, practised by many people around the world, and is itself a product of cultural exchange, having been adapted in the twentieth century by Brazilians who learned Japanese jiu jitsu. There's a considerable gap between respectfully learning from other people and their traditions and turning these traditions into objects for your ridicule, consumption, or commodification. This does not mean martial arts or anything else is free from scrutiny; any given practice could be gross, exploitative, or disrespectful, and each needs to be judged on its own terms. The point is to attune yourself to the way power works structurally and historically as you move through the world and make decisions based on that critical thinking.

Another good example is the international popularity of Indian kurtas, long, loose, collarless shirts that are colourful, beautiful, and comfortable to wear. Kurtas have a long history in South Asia, and now they are sold around the world. Is it an act of appropriation to wear a kurta outside the region where they originated? Is it appropriation for a person to wear one if they are not of South Asian ancestry? India used to clothe the world; prior to British colonization, it dominated the global textile market. Britain bled India of resources, deindustrialized it, and eviscerated its textile industry to build its own. India has a long history of producing beautiful textiles, among many other things, and there's absolutely nothing wrong with people all over the world appreciating that. It's not really about purchasing clothes from one place or another; the issue is with how this production and consumption happens. Everything has a history; everything people make and do is the product of ways of relating to each other and organizing ourselves. These relations are also power relations. There's no neutral position here; ignoring or dismissing these histories and power relations is the same as supporting them. For example, if you're interested in a wearing a kurta or a sari, it's fine to buy one for a fair price. But to avoid looking like Justin Trudeau on a trade mission, you would do well to read a little about the history of the garment and textiles in South Asia. In the process you'll likely develop a genuine interest in much more than a shirt.

Should certain kinds of culturally significant adornment, ritual, and practice be off limits to those outside a cultural group? In a complex world, there can't be any wholesale rejection of ethically partaking in cultures other than your own. But how you go about that matters a great deal. For example, both Alex and Ajay own hoodies and T-shirts designed by Indigenous artists and about various political struggles. We are entirely unconflicted about wearing these items of clothing, even though they feature beautiful and culturally significant images. This is for the simple reason that we were invited to buy, wear, and enjoy them as allies. In many cases these items were part of fund- and awareness-raising campaigns in support of specific and urgent Indigenous struggles. The makers want people to wear them, in no small part to broadcast support for those struggles. It's an act of solidarity but it's also functional (we need clothes) and enjoyable (it's nice to wear things we like). But this solidarity, appreciation, and enjoyment does not give either of us licence to appropriate ceremonial regalia from Indigenous Peoples.

Be thoughtful, nuanced, and aware of the power dynamics animating your ability to access other people's lives and the things they do and have (it's not useful to descend into a self-righteous, alienating, and moralistic lifestyle politics). Ask yourself if the relationship you have with that item or practice is a just one. Is it coming from a place of love? When you're thinking about a question of cultural appropriation or borrowing, it's useful to ask yourself, "Is this a desire to consume or is it a desire to express love?" We don't mean your individual feeling of love, because love is an ongoing relationship. So, if you express love for Black culture, what things are you doing that place you alongside Black communities? What are you doing as an ally or accomplice to uplift Black people? Is the act only about your enjoyment and consumption or does it get humanity a little further down that road to collective liberation by helping people learn from and share with each other? Don't shy away from asking the question and letting the honest answer guide you.

Cancel Everything?

Rather than deal with these admittedly complicated and nuanced power-laden issues squarely, skeptics of concerns about cultural appropriation say that social justice warriors just want to cancel everything. Grandly denouncing what they see as historical revisionism, these skeptics often position themselves as defenders of "viewpoint diversity," "free speech," and even the very roots of Western civilization. Of course, people need opportunities to practise turning ideas over and inspecting them to understand them. Most people are critically reflexive, meaning they are willing to change their point of view about most things when presented with insightful evidence and reasonable argumentation. The irony is that people who bemoan cancel culture as the enemy of freedom are themselves upset when their views are challenged in public. While the person who throws around the term "cancel culture" presents themselves as a champion of the virtues of free speech, it is precisely the *practice* of free speech that invites the charge of cancel culture.

Those defending free speech have historically been marginalized people seeking to gain traction through social movements. Radical left-wing activists, like the Industrial Workers of the World (iww), have

● ● ●

Cancel culture, *noun*
A term commonly used to describe the feeling that leftists or people who identify with progressive politics seek to deplatform and silence anyone who uses harmful and outdated words or ideas. It is popularly used in defences of freedom of speech with no expectation of accuracy or accountability.

been at the forefront of battling for freedom of speech and freedom of assembly. In 1909 the IWW took to the streets to violate a Spokane City Council Ordinance that banned speaking on the streets as a means for the state to help corporations stop workers from organizing with one another. These workers put their bodies on the line to stand on soapboxes and speak while police officers beat them and arrested them by the hundreds for doing it. Ultimately, the IWW was successful in this pivotal fight for free speech. When right-wing movements like the so-called Freedom Convoy of 2022 in Ottawa try to claim the terrain of freedom fighters while stealing food from the homeless and defacing Terry Fox statues, it's important to remember the history.[18]

Statues are a fruitful lens through which to view struggles over power, representation, and history. In well-documented clashes over statues around the world, defenders of the imperial narrative have decried radical leftists or critical race theorists or some other variety of the same for censoring history. This could not be further from the truth. Statues do not author history; they are cultural artifacts established by people with the power to control public space to tell a very particular version of the past. Here in Mi'kma'ki, for example, in 2017, talk of removing a statue of Halifax founder Edward Cornwallis brought organized white supremacists out to attack Indigenous women engaged in ceremony. The statue was erected nearly two hundred years after the founding of Halifax with the explicit aim of making Haligonians feel encouraged about their imperial history during the Great Depression. That fact of history is lost in academic debates about the value of statues, as young white nationalists ignorantly coalesce around a symbol intended to glorify a murderous colonial official who paid established rates for the scalps of Mi'kmaq.

Let's discuss another example about power and representation. In 2021 the estate of the famous children's author Dr. Seuss decided to withdraw six of his books from circulation. The estate did so voluntarily, noting these books contained racist caricatures, particularly of Asian and Black people. This limited culling did not touch any of Dr. Seuss's best-known and enduringly best-selling books. Nevertheless, a chorus of cultural commentators immediately denounced what they saw as an attempt to sanitize the cultural record and cancel Dr. Seuss.

But that isn't what happened. First, to its credit, the estate made this decision without any specific campaign compelling it to act. So who is doing the cancelling? The estate? Second, the Dr. Seuss brand remains immensely popular and lucrative, so this "cancellation" has neither deplatformed Dr. Seuss nor hurt the brand's bottom line. Third, and most important, the six books depicted African and Asian people in outrageously racist ways. No one denied this. Saying these caricatures and the violent legacies they represent are nothing more than products of their time is not a good argument against addressing them now.

If the issue at hand was really free expression and not the defence of unearned privilege, there should be examples of the self-appointed defenders of free speech not only punching down on people objecting to representations that dehumanize them but also punching up when more powerful agents seek to limit these freedoms. Unsurprisingly, these examples are almost impossible to find. For example, when Canada's Parliament passed Bill C-51 in 2015, allowing for the sweeping surveillance of expression across Canadian society, the usual free speech defenders who clutch their pearls about "cancel culture," "historical revisionism," and "political correctness" did not make a peep about this flagrant attack on basic democratic norms. Why? Because they don't actually care about the freedom and responsibility of democratic life; they care about their own privileges and entitlements. They are happy to see the state using its muscle to spy on and repress left radicals and Indigenous people defending their land, who are simplistically cast as "threats" to Canada.

Freedom of speech does not mean that journalists, academics, politicians, entertainers, and other popular culture icons who spew harmful opinions (let's call them "assholes" for simplicity) ought not to be challenged in public. Leaving them unchallenged is not freedom of speech, but freedom from consequences. Put simply, any asshole is entitled to their opinion and their freedom of speech is protected, but if you are going to be a public asshole, you'd better have evidence and reasons. When asshole par excellence Senator Lynn Beyak publicly argued the "benefits" and "good intentions" of the genocidal residential school system were not given adequate airtime in the report of the Truth and Reconciliation Commission, she was given opportunity after opportunity to educate herself on the abysmal history of residential schools and withdraw her baseless argument. Ultimately, she was thrown out of the Conservative caucus and resigned from the Senate in January 2021. Is this an example of being "cancelled" or is it instead an example of an asshole with extreme social and class privilege being coddled by society and still being so far off the mark that even the right-wing party that offered her an unelected seat in government had to remove her?

The majority of newsworthy claims of instances of cancel culture in recent years (think J.K. Rowling, Jordan Peterson, Dave Chappell, Barack Obama, Margaret Atwood, Donald J. Trump) relate to people who have many other public platforms at their disposal. Seeing criticism of them as an affront to free speech also misses the structural dimension of the problem: their public opinions materially harm people. J.K. Rowling's and Dave Chappelle's public transphobia bring nothing new or insightful to the discussion of gender identity. More fundamentally, do the musings of a novelist and a comedian really matter more than the life-and-death struggles faced by gender-nonconforming people? As a Black man in a mixed-race family, Chapelle has overcome incredible structural barriers set up to make him fail, but this does not shield him from being called out when he chooses to be an asshole for profit. Wealthy popular culture icons like Rowling are at no real risk of losing their platforms, but many of the activists and survivors of transphobic hate whose lived reality they dismiss will never have a public platform, because society has already been organized over hundreds of years to defend a facile gender binary as "normal."

There are definitely ways to have these conversations that are moralistic, self-righteous, performative, and alienating (maybe you think we just demonstrated that!). They are not uncommon, and both of us always think deeply about how we can avoid this pitfall. Still, conflicts of this nature don't loom large as a threat to collective social life or basic principles of social justice. Racism *is* such a threat, as are a host of other oppressive relations. Maybe the long walk down the path to collective liberation could begin by dealing with them first.

— ⊕ ——————————————————————————

KEY PRINCIPLE:

Other people's cultures aren't your all-you-can-eat buffet. When oppressed and marginalized people object to the way they are depicted in public, try to consider in good faith their reasons for doing so. Respectful and sincere cultural appreciation, learning, and exchange is possible, necessary, and beautiful, but not on terms set by white supremacy, heteronormativity, settler colonialism, and capitalism.

CAN MEMBERS OF AN OPPRESSED GROUP BE OPPRESSORS?

There's nothing simpler than good and evil, hero and villain, oppressed and oppressor. It's not incidental that "white" and "black" are also binary terms, because the idea of whiteness overlaps with the way people justified colonial expansion as a project of "civilization" — those people closest to a "pure" place (usually Christian Europe) had a right and even obligation to spread purity to the rest of the world. This isn't the whole story of whiteness — far from it — but the idea of a pure, white, honourable, and civilized body opposite a contaminated, black, dishonoured, and uncivilized body helps illustrate not only the problem of thinking in binaries, but also how binary thinking has duped people into excusing and justifying racism and colonialism over the last several hundred years.

Many questions white people ask us are preoccupied with concerns about oppression and anti-oppression that take binary forms, including those about "reverse racism" or the idea that if Europe had not colonized much of the world, someone else would have. In both cases there is an assumption that today's outcome was inevitable, which is ahistorical and works to make the inequities of today appear incidental. In the subtext of their questions, white people often imply that social justice–oriented people assume that white people do not face discrimination and injustice. This is patently untrue, but perhaps it's worth also saying explicitly that racialized people across all intersections and combinations of identities can be spectacular assholes just like white people can. The important thing to remember, as outlined in Chapter 1, is a white person is never being oppressed because of the colour of their skin when they live in a society built upon structural white supremacy. As we explore below, they may be oppressed for a variety of other reasons, and sometimes those oppressing the white person in question may have brown skin. But in this hypothetical situation, the power dynamic between the oppressive nonwhite person and the white person does not exist because of skin colour; it is due to some other form of structural power, such as class, gender, sexuality, or religious position.

Equity Hiring, the Myth of the Meritocracy, and Equal Rights
A common kind of question we are asked in SSFWQ concerns equity and meritocracy in hiring practices. For many, work is the environment in which they most often mix with people not of their choosing, as it is the means through which they sustain themselves and their kin. As a result, white people regularly share concerns about what equity-oriented policy directions may do for their children's

futures — shouldn't the "best qualified" person get the job rather than someone who happens to not be white? The problem lies in the framing of the question, which reveals the person asking it believes they already live in a merit-based society. They don't, and there's much work to be done before such a society can exist.

One of the leading determinants of whether a person goes to university (usually associated with higher lifetime earning potential) is if their parents did. Lots of parents go to great lengths to get their kids into extracurricular activities, paying for horseback riding, golf and hockey lessons, and more. Those kids go on to *look* more well rounded in scholarship applications being read and evaluated by parents who are making the same choices for their children; they see their middle- and upper-class choices mirrored back to them. The kids of parents who have these cultural markers and class status get easier rides through higher education, they get work placements, and then they have better-looking resumes for the job market. As professors who serve a range of students, both of us can easily discern between first-generation university students and those students who come from a family culturally accustomed to university and a middle-class lifestyle. For example, the kids of particularly privileged parents tend to be the ones who have private tutors and at times even legal representatives arguing they didn't plagiarize an assignment. Fundamentally, the likelihood of succeeding in society has a lot more to do with the political, economic, and social privileges a person is born into than it does with their skills, passion, or ability.

Your inheritance — not just money and assets, but the neighbourhood you grew up in, your community spaces, the schools you had access to, the stability of your family home — sets you up to struggle or succeed more than any other indicators. On average, working-class white people in the United States and Canada have amassed far greater inherited wealth than working-class Black or other racialized people, which shows that being white is quite important to whether you will have economic success, more so than intellect or ability.[19] We're not trying to pit working-class white people against working-class nonwhite people — the right-wing populist hellscape of much of the industrial world right now shows how that kind of politics can be weaponized. Part of the problem with a lot of the language around equity, diversity, inclusion, and accessibility (EDIA) in the workplace is that it does not go far enough in connecting with the status quo situation of an unfair concentration of wealth and power in the hands of a largely white, male, overprivileged class that writes, debates, and rules on laws that shape society. It encourages people who are marginalized by many systems simultaneously (including white people) to find conflict with one another in a divide-to-rule politics with deep roots in colonial capitalism.

If you want to live in an equal society, you must settle your historical accounts. You are not just an individual; you are the sum of everyone who has come before you, shaping a society that treats people differently. When an employer makes a case for equity-based hiring, some are quick to dismiss it as the collapse of "merit," without coming to terms with how the last five hundred years have arguably been the greatest affirmative action project for the advancement of mediocre white men. (We know there are lots of brilliant, hard-working white men. Relax!) Feminists and nonwhite people have been arguing this for centuries. Just because politicians and commentators love to talk about multicultural Canada being the best place in the world does not mean we live in an equal society. Deep and foundational inequities are woven into the fibres of this country. Even Papa Trudeau's book was called *Towards a Just Society*, not *We're Loving Our Just Society!*

More examples? In a just society where everyone competed equally and with a reasonably fair starting point, nonwhite children would not worry about being shot by fearful white people on transit or followed around like thieves in stores, while white kids carrying pipe bombs into airports were unproblematically allowed to travel. These are not hypothetical scenarios. Eighteen-year-old Sammy Yatin was shot to death in 2013 by law enforcement while alone on a Toronto streetcar, holding a small blade and likely having a mental health episode, even though a nonlethal option (a Taser) was en route. In contrast, eighteen-year-old Skylar Murphy brought a fully function-ing pipe bomb into Edmonton International Airport in 2014 but was allowed to continue on his trip to Mexico. Security believed he didn't want to blow up a plane because he seemed surprised when confronted about the pipe bomb. He was only arrested upon his return. A scolding judge gave him a fine, which he tried to pay by selling his side of the story to the media. The vastly different experi-ences of these eighteen-year-olds tell a critical story about how race affects how society perceives threats. Both teenagers had weapons, and any reasonable person would agree that suitable punishment ought to have landed somewhere between the white treatment and the brown treatment. Authorities saw no threat in Skylar's white body and no value in Sammy's brown body.

When employers try to hire from equity-deserving groups, this too is a bit of a smokescreen. The employer recognizes a structural deficiency stemming from systematically undervaluing people who are not white cis men. Now, because of decades of social justice organizing by activists across a variety of lived experiences in society, it is no longer culturally popular for men to relegate women colleagues to supporting roles or to throw out applications of "hard to pronounce" names. (They still do it, but it's gotta be more hush-hush. If you think we're exaggerating, ask your Asian friends why they have an "English" name or ask your Aunty about the joys of office life.) The point is that the failure and duty to correct is on the part of employers — the failure is not the fault or responsibility of people who have been systematically discriminated against. Efforts aimed at recruiting and retaining a greater diversity of workers are about improving the institution by enriching it with people who bring value from their lived experiences paired with their professional credentials. Diversity is a core competency most employers lack; having a diversity of employees corrects this deficiency — not because they are from nondominant backgrounds alone, but because they are at least equally qualified on traditional metrics *plus* bring lived experience with them.

Even with equity-based hiring, there are limitations that need to be worked out. Simply checking a box and saying "Yes, I am a member of an equity-seeking group" has proven to be problematic. We would love, instead, if *all* candidates for jobs were asked to think about their inheritance, broadly speaking. Sometimes this is called "positionality," which connects a person's lived experience to the work they intend to do. This is something white people in particular have comparatively little experience with, and we have found it makes them more uncomfortable than it does others (though plenty of nonwhite people are uncomfortable with it too). But if everyone comes to terms with how they are the products of lots of inheritances they did not choose, society will the better for it.

Here's a personal example to help make the point. Ajay joined the faculty at Dalhousie University as part of a diversity hiring line, in which candidates had to be from an equity-deserving group. As a result, he has spent hours patiently explaining to reporters and trolls, "No, in fact I am not occupying a position a better-qualified white man should have. The university correctly understood that my lived experience combines with my equal or better professional experience to inform my work." To be hired on the premise of diversity is to have society see you as fundamentally undeserving, even while you are expected to do copious amounts of extra work to help transform your institution, be it a law firm, a retail store, a hospital, a fire department, or a university. This behind-the-scenes service work, which many institutions do not

* * *

Positionality, *noun*
A way of understanding the importance of one's lived experience and how it affects how one moves through the world. It explains how people may not immediately notice or understand things that are everyday experiences for others.

value (materially or otherwise), is a kind of work that white cis men are neither expected nor asked to do. Part of the legacy of historic under-representation of racialized people in institutions — any institution, take your pick — means the handful of us who are there shoulder the responsibility to represent our communities, mentor racialized or otherwise nondominant students, and provide emotional labour to colleagues and bosses who are uncomfortable discussing race, all in an effort to make an inclusive and equal society. Even though the steps taken have been small, these minor successes serve as the basis of attacks from predominantly (but not entirely) white people who choose to believe white men have not been historically advantaged.

One of the best things you can do as a white person interested in working against structural racism is to volunteer to do as much institutional EDIA work as you can, so your racialized colleagues are not doing all this work. Stepping up and doing this work is a transformative opportunity — especially for people without the lived experience of multiple forms of marginalization — when approached with an open and curious mind. Reach out to your racialized colleagues when you need some input, by all means. Build horizontal alliances and encourage people to think about their positionalities. In our experience it is often easier to connect with white women than it is with white men while doing this work, because cis men benefit from the unearned privilege of patriarchy. Women, including white women, generally have experienced the bullshit of patriarchy in every aspect of their life, and so are often ready to understand that similar forms of bullshit, such as racism, are equally endemic.

But beware the potential double-speak of EDIA work — the *i* is the trickiest part of it, because inclusion in an institution that is not yet ready, willing, and excited to fundamentally change itself is doomed to fail. Many employers *want* EDIA initiatives to fail as long as it says they tried on paper; they will commit insufficient resources to what they see as a "nice to have" but "not essential" piece of work. If your employer asks you or someone you know to strike a committee, be sure to ask them what resources and institutional changes they are prepared to entertain. And get it in writing, lest you waste your time.

If you find yourself in a tough conversation with folks who really need to "tell it like it is" and you need to expose the illusion of meritocracy, present them with this: if society is mostly equal yet still has a 30 percent wage gap between men and women and a gross overrepresentation of white men in all the powerful places in society, the only logical conclusion is there is something innately superior about white men relative to the rest of society. Even your white male bosses should agree with you that, well, there's a problem.

Lateral Violence, Migrants, and Settlers

Privilege and oppression alike can manifest in really obvious ways, as the examples of Sammy Yatim and Skylar Murphy demonstrate, but at other times they are hard to see. Homophobia and ageism, for example, can cause everyday oppression but may also intersect with some structural forms of privilege (like having wealth, being able-bodied, etc.). They may also intersect with structural forms of disadvantage, like being racialized. Even communities that appear at face value to be homogeneous never really are. The idea of the "good ol'

Canadian town" with the Zamboni in the Tim Horton's commercials is a nationalist caricature that generally scripts rural Canada in binary opposition to urban Canada, stripping both of the complexity and nuances that give life meaning.

Let's take a minute to talk about representation. Most people tend to think that when someone from an identifiably marginalized group says something, it is broadly representative of the group, and this is a significant mistake. There isn't a Black or Botswanan position on anything. Such uniform agreement is impossible and undesirable; however, the pervasive expectation that any member of a marginalized community can stand in for it is so common it goes unspoken most of the time. Asking your Black friend about Colin Kaepernick taking a knee does not reveal the "Black" position on taking a knee in sports. Rarely would anyone think to ask a white person about the white position on knee taking, because it is more readily understood that white people have a wide range of views.

Oppression sometimes remains invisible or difficult to perceive when lateral violence happens across people and communities. For example, people of South Asian ancestry may also be complicit in anti-Black racism, participate in the ongoing settler-colonial displacement of Indigenous Peoples from their lands, and even enact violence against other South Asians through Islamophobia, casteism, and more. This is not to pick on South Asians, but both of us have South Asian roots so it's useful to draw from this experience. When there is racial lateral violence at play, such as East Asians and South Asians employing racial slurs and perpetuating stereotypes about one another, it can be useful to turn to historical examples of what solidarity has looked like in the real world. For example, the camaraderie between Zhou Enlai and Jawaharlal Nehru, prime ministers of the fledgling postcolonial nations of China and India, respectively, tells a story of struggle to overcome modes of empire.

Another way lateral violence can emerge in ways not directly related to race is regarding the differences between displaced migrants such as refugees and settlers. Especially in the wake of recent refugee migrations from Ukraine (opposite historical settler migrations), Syria, and Afghanistan, it is worth keeping in mind these definitions: A migrant is a person who arrives somewhere new and then works hard to learn how to integrate themselves into what is there. A settler, on the other hand, is a person who arrives and tries to re-create the home and dismantle what is already there.[20] A glance around Canada shows how this story unfolds — cities named Kingston or Victoria, legal systems built on French and English traditions, and many streets and monuments dedicated to imperialists like Edward Cornwallis.

Refugees, in our opinion, are not settlers in the same way as are white settlers who came to build Canada overtop of the many Indigenous Peoples that have always been here. There are a variety of reasons for this, perhaps most centrally the precarious legal status of refugees and undocumented people more generally, who are often displaced and made to move because of the actions of wealthy and predominantly white countries.[21] The kind of welcome refugees receive is often affected by their race and religion, which in turn impacts public perception of what makes a "desirable" refugee. This mirrors much of the racism of Canadian immigration policy over the last 150 years.[22] It has also created the context in which refugees who have been present in Canada for a long time have, in some important instances, sought to close the door on new refugees. In these unfortunate situations, pandering to settler-colonial nationalism creates material rewards, fuelling forms of lateral violence.

We would wager a shiny dollar that most people on earth are of mixed ancestry. With the knowledge there is no scientific basis for "race," mixed ancestry is really a question about people's genealogies, the twists and turns culminating in their existence. Nevertheless, a society organized by structural white supremacy continues to view mixed ancestry involving whiteness as a form of "contamination," which helps explain many of the racial slurs that exist for biracial and multiracial people. In racial thinking, whiteness and blackness are about purity and impurity; white people are not actually white and Black people are actually not black. The binary captures the ideology of white supremacy and helps illuminate the historical processes through which some people have "become" white, and how being anything but white has historically been treated as less human. Racial oppression isn't only about how white culture and ideas are treated as "normal" and others are treated as "different." Lateral violence happens for a number of reasons, and an important one in settler-colonial societies like Canada is that people copy colonial behaviours and sensibilities in an attempt to achieve inclusion and integration in the settler colony.

Privilege: It's in You to Use!

We started this chapter by saying anyone could be an oppressor and anyone could be oppressed, but not always in the same way. Breaking down the white supremacist objective of having blood or race purity involves everyone claiming all of who they are. Own the fullness of your identity and recognize that having a connection to European or South Asian or East African culture and tradition is much, much deeper than race alone. This is not an easy task for most people, especially Indigenous people, many of whom have had to hide their Indigenous ancestry to avoid violent settler-colonial attempts to seize children and incarcerate them in prisons masquerading as schools over most of Canadian history. It is similarly challenging for survivors of slavery and indentureship who often cannot trace any records of where their ancestors originated.

Getting to know your history is important. The deplorable conditions of the European working class drove masses of them to Canada and other parts of the western hemisphere — the so-called new world — and then into conditions of structural racial conflict with the people whose lands were being stolen as well as people who were enslaved. Despite what politicians or podcast hosts or fragile academics might want to lead the public to believe, slavery and genocide were foundational pillars of modern Canada. Racial conflict has transformed, but it has never ended, and the descendants of these different kinds of people in Canada are still in conflict.[23] Even "owning" property on stolen territory forces those privileged enough to have exited impossible rental markets to grapple with complicity. When you are of mixed ancestry this can be extra challenging, especially if you are, for instance, of African and Mi'kmaw descent living in Algonquin territory. If your ancestors happen to be from Europe and you are white or white-passing, consider the kind of access and safety you have in certain situations, which your darker-skinned friends may not have, and try to step up and into useful roles accordingly. In our estimation, privilege is not something to be scorned or lamented. As we continue to argue in the next chapter, privilege ought to be used as best as possible to fight for a world in which it does not exist.

K E Y   P R I N C I P L E :

Beware of binary thinking and how thinking in "black and white" terms compels you to sacrifice context. Claim all of who you are and use the privileges you have for positive social change.

CHAPTER 8

HOW CAN WHITE PEOPLE BE INVOLVED IN ANTIRACIST STRUGGLES WITHOUT CENTRING THEMSELVES?

Make no mistake, white people are critical to defanging and ultimately defeating white supremacy. The question is how. Particularly in white-dominated societies, mobilizing at least a significant minority of white people in pursuit of antiracist and collective liberation struggles is a necessary step in advancing them. However, knowing how essential it is still doesn't provide much direction on the best ways to do this. There are lots of models for advancing social justice and social change — what principles can be used to navigate this crowded field and avoid pitfalls? Perhaps most importantly, how can white people become meaningfully involved in antiracist struggles without centring whiteness and themselves?

No Saviours, No Penitents

As activists, organizers, and teachers, both of us have seen lots of examples of well-meaning white people attend social justice events and embody two equally problematic positions: the saviour and the penitent. The saviour shows up with lots of information and answers. Brimming with zeal and confidence, they have some knowledge about the issues at hand. But rather than humbly contributing to the larger collective organizing process, they are unfailingly sure they know how to fix the problem and not shy about taking up space to assert this. On the flip side, the penitent shows up riddled with guilt and shame, desperately seeking comfort and absolution. The penitent feels their own complicity in dominant power relations very deeply and is desperate to publicly confess this and be released from their existential burden.

Not only are these positions obnoxious (no one likes a know-it-all or a martyr), they also centre whiteness and white people in contexts and struggles that are not really about them. The saviour and the penitent are like sinkholes, sucking in everything around them, and actually serve to inhibit rather than amplify struggles for social change. The saviour wants pride of place, they want to lead, to give the answers, to fix the problem. If only people would just listen to them! The penitent takes every opportunity to express their sadness and regret, making themselves the needy centre of a conversation not about them.

Though the saviour and the penitent seem like polar opposites, they are both expressions of structural white supremacy. They centre whiteness in spaces and processes that are supposed to be about other people and their struggles. They expect and demand recognition from racialized people rather than just participate in a collective process of trying to change the world. Thankfully, the key to avoiding this particular pitfall is pretty basic. If you're a white person looking to become involved in antiracist struggles, start by just showing up consistently at events and helping out with whatever needs doing without expecting to be recognized for it. Show up. Be humble. Do the work. Doing the work can take a lot of different forms. Maybe it's helping set up or tear down for a meeting, event, or rally. Maybe it's helping out with food preparation and childcare. Maybe it's providing access to resources.

When Ajay first moved back to Mi'kma'ki (specifically, Nova Scotia) after being away for ten years, activists had initiated a campaign to remove a statue of Halifax's founder, Edward Cornwallis. (You've met Eddie C. before, as we've mentioned him several times in the book). Ajay didn't yet have good connections in Halifax and had not yet built relations with local Indigenous struggles and communities. He supported the campaign and wanted to be involved but didn't want to take up space and present himself as some kind of expert with all the answers. So he turned up at a couple events, and then in advance of a large planned protest at the Cornwallis statue, he and his partner made several hundred "solidarity pakoras." The day of the demonstration, they set up shop and made the pakoras available by donation, with all the money going to the event organizers. As a side benefit, Ajay and his partner also engaged in an act of cultural exchange and appreciation by introducing Mi'kmaw Elders in attendance to vegetable pakoras. Without knowing how they would be received, they came with something to offer, and in doing so made a meaningful cultural connection and contributed tangibly to the struggle. If you turn up and do the work needed, people will eventually notice you and begin to trust you.

Make Your Privilege Work against White Supremacy
If you're a white person who doesn't know many racialized people, then talk to other white people about racial justice. Open up those spaces. As a white person working in a primarily white space, you can work to make it less racist and help other white people see and question white supremacy. This is important. Many racialized activists and organizers are asked time and again to show up at political events organized by white people and for a primarily white audience to do the necessary work of awareness raising and popular education. It's not hard to see how this places the burden yet again on marginalized and oppressed groups. As a white person, engaging and educating other white people about racism and racial justice is work you can readily do. Think about how you can make use of your privilege in pursuit of collective liberation. Thinking about privilege as a tool to be wielded is a lot more useful than seeing it as a burden to carry. This isn't going to get you out of having to account for a life shaped by unearned, unjust, and undeserved privileges, but guilt will only silence you while making you no less complicit in the relations that produce it. Instead, wherever possible, find ways to direct that unearned racialized privilege towards educating other white people about social justice and undermining toxic relations.

If you're getting together with others to organize for some social justice struggle, do so in as open and welcoming a way as possible. Building an inclusive and diverse crew of activists for making change over the long haul is a great goal. But if your group is more homogeneous in terms of identity, don't try to force diversity. Organize where you are in the spirit of solidarity and justice, and then find those connections while you build. Seek out organizations of racialized people and see what you can do to work together, but don't simply try to add their members to your group, because that would tokenize people. Making social change is not like baking; you can't just add diversity and mix. Racialized and oppressed communities are heterogeneous, diverse, and complicated, as we discussed in Chapter 7. It's easy to project a uniformity and purity onto experiences you don't intimately understand, but it's vital to understand every human community as a complex, contradictory, and diverse place. If you're looking for neat little groups of saints and sinners, you're in for a surprise.

There's no better way to do grassroots antiracist work than by offering to be part of the solutions already posed by people who are directly affected by racism. Men do not need to save women from the patriarchy, straight people do not need to save queer folks from homophobia, and white people do not need to save racialized people from racism. Falling into the trap of thinking this way will land you right back on the teeth of the saviour complex. Each liberation struggle is bound up with every other one. When one struggle for justice breaks through, everyone gets a little freer. Ending white supremacy and racism will not just help racialized people live freer from violence, it will help white people too. When individuals with all their diverse identities refuse to be conscripted any longer into reproducing oppression, when they stop being tools in ruling class domination, they recover their humanity.

Start basically and practically. If you're looking to make connections and learn more about racialized people's liberation struggles, does your group have the capacity to offer honoraria to invited speakers? Members of oppressed groups are frequently asked to do all kinds of education work, even informally, which can constitute a real burden in their lives. When you're not living your life up against the cutting edges of structural violence and you're coming from a place of goodwill, it's hard to understand how off-putting it is to be constantly asked to show up at white-dominated events, educate, and provide acceptable suggestions for allyship. It feels like just another way of saying, "Tell me what to do, I'll do it, this will be over, and then I can stop feeling guilty about it."

Offering some form of remuneration is not about turning activism into paid work, and it's not about white guilt. It's about recognizing the material costs paid by activists and groups in driving social change, and contributing to meeting them. Reach out to the social justice groups around you who are already doing this work and ask them if they could suggest speakers who might be willing to visit you and your crew to talk about a specific issue. If you can offer a modest honorarium, make sure to mention this. Don't ask them to tell you what to do. That's just putting the burden of liberation back on their shoulders. The task is to build ways of relating to each other that allow us to be accomplices and co-conspirators in a struggle for collective liberation.[24] Well-intentioned white people can do a lot that is not tokenistic and involves engaging the knowledge that comes out of oppressed communities.

Don't Grift

Don't be a grifter. Don't enter spaces looking to maximize your own profit. That goes for not just white people but for anyone entering social justice work with the intention of building their brand and padding their résumé. Unfortunately, we have lots of examples of individuals and groups, with the best of intentions or not, that monopolize platforms, attention, and resources while claiming the exclusive right to speak for a larger group of which they might be a part. Nothing good comes from treating social change work like an industry you're seeking a competitive advantage in.

This applies especially to attempts to accrue social capital. If the reason you're engaged in activism is because you want to be seen to be doing the right thing, then you should step back, take a deep breath, and reorient yourself. It's not about you being seen. The world does not need another influencer. It's about doing the work. Be active in your society. Challenge those relations, ways of being, and institutions that perpetuate violence and make people's lives unlivable. Don't speak for other people; they can speak for themselves. You can engage with movements — they exist in the world; they're meant to be engaged. That doesn't mean you should try to lead them. You can and should have conversations with

•   •   •

Collective liberation, *noun*
Freedom for all, understood in the sense that no one is really free until everyone is, and one group's liberation cannot come at the cost of another's. It also embodies the notion that each struggle against oppression and exploitation is part of a much bigger constellation of freedom struggles.

all kinds of people about how to challenge racism and white supremacy. Don't self-segregate based on some puritanical notion of identity politics. People are most vulnerable when they retreat to their enclaves.

Simply put, other people's struggles for justice and liberation are not your career opportunity. It's tempting to manifest your political and ethical commitments in the world through your waged work. Those from society's middle class, in particular, are frequently reminded that they should find value and meaning in their work. A lot has been said about the problems with the mushroom-like growth of the not-for-profit industrial complex.[25] All too often, nongovernmental organizations (NGOs) act as a bureaucratic lid on the boiling pot of social unrest. Instead of empowering oppressed communities, NGOs are, like all bureaucratic organizations, often just invested in perpetuating themselves. After all, ending the problem your organization was formed to address would mean the end of the organization. That's a bit harsh, but it's fair to say many NGOs are gatekeepers to scarce resources and enforcers of a kind of respectability politics, judging what meets the cut of acceptable activism and social change. Respectability politics are more than reputational; they offer a vital public tool for the ruling class to defuse and demobilize grassroots

• • •

Respectability politics, *noun*
A form of political gatekeeping that demands people's struggles for social justice and social change conform to the norms and values of dominant society. This insistence on abiding by prevailing standards of civility disciplines and limits liberation struggles.

struggle by casting certain kinds of struggles as illegitimate and even criminal, terroristic, or traitorous.

There's also something dangerously mystifying about the way NGOs, charities, and other advocacy organizations approach social justice issues. Often because of the way laws require them to operate and be structured to maintain charitable status, tax exemptions, and access to grants and other forms of funding, each of these organizations specializes in some specific aspect of social injustice and suffering (e.g., child soldiers, global hunger, fair trade, child and maternal health, anti-oppression training). The problem with this is that unless people are talking about the way oppression and exploitation intertwine in society, they are only seeing a part of the puzzle. Worse than this, by hiving off into discrete areas of focus, the not-for-profit industrial

● ● ●

Not-for-profit industrial complex, *noun*
The array of nonprofit, nongovernmental organizations that claim to address a variety of social justice issues but whose existence is tied to the perpetuation of the problem they claim to confront. This system can often function, intentionally and not, to inhibit rather than empower struggles for social change by guarding access to scarce resources, expertise, and political legitimacy.

Unconscious bias, *noun*
The false notion that oppression in society emerges from the biases, assumptions, preferences, and prejudices each person carries around inside their heads. From this perspective, forms of oppression like racism and sexism can only be fixed by by having individuals work on themselves to recognize these biases and minimize their impact on decision-making. It entirely sidelines how oppression and exploitation intertwine, how they are entrenched in dominant social institutions, and how they organize social relations.

complex actually perpetuates the status quo. An exclusive focus on one form of oppression risks turning social justice struggles into purely technical issues requiring only the right tweaks to life made by experts. This kind of approach reduces oppression to rule-governed bureaucracy and human relations training. It leads to the dead end of corporate "diversity and inclusion" and "unconscious bias" training. While highly lucrative for the ranks of professional consultants, these approaches actually do harm to efforts to achieve greater justice by getting individuals to think about and work on things that are not transformative. They inhibit analyses of how the dehumanization of groups of people makes possible a world where some people can live off the lives and labour of others. It's imperative to confront the material reasons for and consequences of groups of people being dispossessed, degraded, and exploited for the benefit of others. This understanding has to be at the core of antiracist work.

KEY PRINCIPLE:

If you are a white person looking to be involved in antiracist work, don't try to be a saviour, don't wallow in penitence, and most definitely do not turn it into a grift. Find ways to turn your unearned privilege into a tool to dismantle white supremacy and prioritize educating and organizing other white people as part of a wider struggle for collective liberation.

HOW CAN I BE AN ANTIRACIST IN MY EVERYDAY LIFE?

Once upon a time, Yaja was a federal public servant in a mythical land called Adanac. He was told by a superior during a research meeting that the sure-fire way to prevent the smuggling of illegal goods at the land border was to search trucks driven by South Asians. Yaja chuckled at first, thinking this was just another racist microaggression masquerading as a joke, but Bossman was adamant. As the argument heated up, Yaja frustratedly said, "You can't write a turban hunt into federal law!" Bossman was incensed at the thinly veiled suggestion that singling out truckers by race could be seen as racist; from his perspective, the idea came from a career of observation and experience. That he and his mostly white colleagues might be racially profiling people at the border was a novel and unwelcome insight.

We start this chapter with Yaja's story not because of the Bossman's behaviour but because of what was happening in the background. This was a team-based research policy meeting related to international border security. As Yaja relays the story to us, when things got heated, not a single colleague in the room spoke up. They shuffled papers, looked at their shoes, and exchanged worried glances. Later, at the photocopier, they confided in Yaja: they respected that he had stood up against what was obviously racism, but for one reason or another, they could not risk saying anything. Yaja resigned from the public service shortly after, thinking in his youthful naivete that problems of this nature were unique to government work. He has since found similar (albeit less dramatic) everyday instances of structural oppression in all forms of work he has engaged in.

White people often ask for guidance about what it takes to be an antiracist in their everyday lives. It's a great question to get, because to pose a question in this way implies the person asking understands that when society is organized by racism, there is no scenario in which one can simply be "nonracist." We discussed problems associated with binary thinking in previous chapters, but one of the few areas where it makes sense is in deciding to be racist or antiracist. As antiracist historian Ibram X. Kendi tweeted in 2019, "Racism is death. Antiracism is life." Life and death are very big issues, and for white people looking to dip a toe into antiracist organizing, there are lots of small steps and everyday practices you can put in place to help you on your path towards dismantling racism. We dedicate this chapter to sharing our best practices, but readers should know that lots of writers across various racial backgrounds have shared their stories and best practices for committing to antiracism.[26] Here's what works for us.

CHAPTER 9

Embracing Discomfort
People are naturally wired to avoid things that hurt them or make them feel uncomfortable. Discomfort is an important feeling, and when you approach it with curiosity and a willingness to educate yourself, it is the basis upon which all other forms of learning can take place. Try to develop a habit of dwelling in discomfort. Read books and novels written by racialized people about their experiences and dedicate some time each day or once a week to reflect on what you are learning. This could take the form of just thinking things through in your head before you go to bed, or maybe you prefer to keep a journal or mull things over during a fifteen-minute walk with your stoic dog. (Never underestimate the therapeutic value of long conversations with dogs!) The point is to begin to notice when you feel uncomfortable with the topic of race and racism, and then consciously choose to remain uncomfortable rather than leave the stress-inducing situation.

Feeling guilty or choosing to be silent (like Yaja's colleagues) in a stressful situation related to racism are manifestations of what white scholar Robin DiAngelo has famously described as "white fragility." Lots of racialized scholars have described this phenomenon in different

● ● ●

White fragility, *noun*
The feelings of guilt, anger, and defensiveness experienced and expressed by white people when confronted with situations in which they are forced to understand themselves in racial terms. Popularized by Robin DiAngelo, the term also describes how resources are often redeployed to care for white people's feelings rather than deal with the harm done to nonwhite people.

99

ways, but many white people have been extremely open to hearing this message told through the narrative that DiAngelo offers.[27] To be sure, white writers are afforded more space and attention than racialized ones saying the same things, but both of us find DiAngelo's work to be useful because it helps white people get a foot in the door of thinking about racial justice and injustice. So read DiAngelo's work, but make sure you also read lots of work by nonwhite experts on race and racism too.

Break the Inertia of Racism

Once you have done some reading and introspection, your confidence or at least your curiosity will grow as well. Look for racism in your everyday life. We don't mean neo-Nazis marching in the street. Canada does have a large and growing problem with fascists and far-right white supremacists and open Nazis — despite mainstream media's astonishment about this, the country has always had this problem. But most folks are not going to be the ones tasked with fighting violent white supremacists of this nature, and paying too much attention to smaller groups of openly racist people only serves the purpose of lulling the public into the false sense that they live in a "nonracist" society. Most racism is subtler.

You may not find yourself in a situation as dramatic as Yaja's, but we promise you there are examples of everyday structural racism happening at your place of employment right now (behind you!).[28] Sometimes these are subtle, and the subtlety is often grounded in actions that people feel they have no control over. The philosopher Jacques Rancière says that true democratic politics happens not necessarily through movement but through stoppages. When the forces of society notice people are shocked en masse by something outrageous, they usher people along, saying, "Move on, there's nothing to see here." But those who refuse to move along, who stand in place and force a break in the inertia of "normal" society, are the ones enacting politics by forcing others to pay attention to precisely what they do not wish to see.[29]

Try this at work, at the dinner table, or on the bus. For example, someone we know was the only South Asian person in their workplace, and a colleague insisted on asking them questions about turmeric every day. As people of South Asian descent, we understand that many white people are coming around to what our ancestors understood to be medicine and food, and we are happy enough to have a conversation about turmeric. The concern at our friend's workplace was the frequency with which this conversation emerged, which should have prompted another white colleague to take the turmeric sleuth aside and say, "Listen pal, you can find lots of information about turmeric on the ol' internets." The turmeric sleuth likely did not see themselves as being engaged in any form of racism; after all, they were appreciating what they saw as a cultural characteristic of the South Asian region. But they were reducing their South Asian colleague to one part of that person's identity while acting as though they were entitled to turmeric secrets from that colleague (who was probably just trying to finish their report and get the heck outta Dodge to go rock climbing or learn about ethnic food like hot dogs). A useful intervention in this ordinary, everyday example of racism could take the form of another white person stepping in to do some gentle education with the white colleague, saving the racialized person from the daily microaggressions.

Normalize Discomfort for Others

Part of the everyday work you can do after a bit of reading, reflection, and observation is to take small steps like intervening in the great turmeric inquisition. Importantly, these kinds of actions also make the discomfort of intervening in everyday forms of racism seem more normal for the other white people in your life. (We advise white people to avoid doing this kind of intervention with nonwhite people in their lives. Leave those necessary interventions to other nonwhite people, unless you are close friends with the person or in a position of authority where you have to intervene.) Normalizing discomfort for others can be done with a smile on your face and a matter-of-fact disposition. You don't need to have a solution to a problem to draw attention to the problem. Sometimes the solution emerges out of the discussion that ensues when you intervene. Patriarchy and racism are insidious because they occupy and structure perceptions of "normal" and make it easy for people to justify them: "Oh my grandmother is from a different time. She doesn't mean what she said about Jewish people," or "In my household we divide 'blue' and 'pink' labour because it's easier for us to operate that way." It is easier to go along with the inertia of society, but it's not necessarily better.

Pay attention to what kinds of jokes your kids are making. Gently intervene, if you need to, to help them understand that making light of race is part of the way kids get socialized to learn racism and see it as a "normal" rather than abhorrent part of everyday life. Teaching your kids about race before they learn about feeling uncomfortable having difficult conversations will set them up to succeed. It's kind of like administering a vaccine — they may still internalize society's racism, but they will be much better equipped to fight it if they have at least partial protection from early conversations about race and seeing their families model behaviour that challenges inertia. No one is born racist; it is a learned condition that must be unlearned.

Weaponize Your Privilege

We've come back to this point several times in this book — privilege needs to be used. Like learning a martial art, becoming an antiracist is a lifelong commitment, but one that allows huge leaps in your learning and practice in the early days. In six months, you could probably go from embracing discomfort and practising introspection to noticing what's happening around you and intervening, to normalizing discomfort for others around you, to the essential step of weaponizing your privilege. We hear from many white people who feel unable to act in support of antiracism because they are aware that whiteness takes up too much space in society and space must be made for marginalized voices. We agree there's a need for marginalized voices and leadership, but racism is a fundamental problem for and of whiteness; therefore, white people need to be the backbone of antiracist efforts. This does not mean white people need to be in leadership positions, although we know, for the most part, they are.

Whiteness holds a privileged position in society. The image of a "normal" Canadian citizen has been constructed over hundreds of years of policy development, colonization, and white supremacy of a direct and indirect nature. If you are working towards being a dedicated antiracist, you should use the privileges you have, whether they are earned or unearned, and weaponize them effectively to create institutional and political change. Yaja's story happened fifteen years ago; it's unlikely that racism would take such an obvious and odious form today as it did then (Win?!). But now, as then, more white people need to speak up publicly in the moment, instead of privately afterward, so policy and other outcomes turn out better.

Deciding to use your white privilege in defence of the efforts of nonwhite friends and colleagues can make a huge difference because of the unearned privilege your whiteness offers you. This is not something to be lamented or a source of shame, which we hear about from white people in SSFWQ with great frequency. If you are jumped in a dark alley, or see someone being jumped in a dark alley, you should not be afraid or ashamed to use whatever means you have at your disposal to fight. Kendi was not being metaphorical when he said antiracism is life and racism is death. And the truth is, white people do not face the same level of punishment from the state for acting in defence of movements like Black Lives Matter or Indigenous sovereignty, so in all likelihood you will not face much or any consequences from authorities.

Overstepping your position may draw consequences from those you seek to work with though, and it's important not to enact white saviourism (see Chapter 8) when you start dipping your toes into antiracist action. Turning up and learning is important not just for you but for the people and organizations fighting for racial justice as well. They learn that you can be trusted. If your level of commitment is just coming to a protest or rally, they don't need to develop much trust in you — and if that is your comfort level, then do that, and everyone will be happy for it. But as you want to get further and further involved, you can take some steps to help communicate that you are there to support.

Using the example of public protests or education campaigns, if you see something that looks interesting and want to help out, get in touch with the organizers and say you're willing to help. Even better is if you can bring something thoughtful to the table so organizers don't have to find a task for you. Perhaps you can offer to organize coffee and tea donations from a local coffee shop and bring them to the event. Maybe you can make sandwiches (try to be inclusive of various dietary requirements); maybe you can help with childcare at the site; or you could be the point person talking to the cops and city if a permit is required to gather. Be a march marshal if you are marching, so your body is between any potential disturbance and the racialized organizers. We have seen white allies deploying these tactics with great success, and in the process, relationships are built. Solidarity is a verb: it is not a state of being, it is being in the act.

Not everyone is going to be comfortable getting involved in antiracist organizing, and that is absolutely okay. If your threshold is educating yourself to better understand why nonwhite people are fighting for their lives under structural white supremacy, that is valuable. And if you can talk to other white people about what you have learned, that is also valuable. The next step does not have to take the form of political organizing, because everyday, nothin'-fancy public interventions can be affirming for people under attack and also educational for the silent white majority. Take for example racism or sexism (or most frequently, racism and sexism at the same time) occurring on public transit. This happens all the time, and women of colour seem to be the chief targets for a variety of structural reasons. White people can respond in ways that can be very impactful. We have seen white people feign solidarity with a white aggressor by trying to take them aside and "call them in" as a form of de-escalation. We have also seen white people get right up in the face of a racist and escort them off a bus for their behaviour. That second example can be effective, but please remember to centre the person enduring the assault and not your desire to act because of the outrage you are (correctly) feeling when you see racist attacks unfolding. Maybe they're tuning it out because this is their everyday and they simply cannot get worked up about every bit of bullshit they encounter and remain functional. Still, there's nothing wrong in sitting next to them to break the line of sight with the person making racist or sexist comments, and then checking in to see if they are okay or would like some direct support. Maybe just engage them in conversation and create a space for the situation to de-escalate on its own. Not everything needs to be dramatic. Everyone benefits when antiracism becomes normal instead of exceptional.

Take Direction Graciously

Finally, it's really important to emphasize again that as you move towards being antiracist in your everyday life, you will make mistakes. As outlined in Chapter 2, try to make good mistakes. Don't show up and try to steer the conversation or strategize in a direction you think is right, even if what you think is right might be a great course of action. Social change is not a linear process, and it is as much about transformation through practice as it is about end goals. Ajay fondly reflects on a critical lesson he learned from one of his white friends and allies, Chris Dixon, during a street protest against Islamophobia in Ottawa. Chris gently encouraged Ajay to "spend time with the megaphone," which Ajay was not particularly keen to do as he preferred to look after behind-the-scenes logistics. But the broader social context of movement-based education and transformation meant, in spending time with the megaphone, Ajay had an opportunity to develop a different skill set, which is to his individual benefit but also to the benefit of movements in which he participates.

Take direction from those with more experience than you. Sometimes the way that direction comes out won't be polite, and it might make you feel bad; however, usually it happens not because an organizer, colleague, or friend is trying to hurt your feelings but because they are pressed into a tight spot and urgently need you to do or not do something. Being a white ally can mean stepping back rather than stepping forward, for political and structural reasons, not personal ones. Being a good ally and antiracist means acting in ways that might make you uncomfortable because you are committed to practising solidarity as a verb. For instance, in the case someone says unkind and untrue things about you in a public meeting, you have to decide how to react. When we have been in situations like this, we have found the best course of action is often to say nothing and yield the space to others. When people who are stressed to their breaking points are forced to organize against the life-and-death consequences of racism, they might snap from time to time. Prioritize their well-being, always look for the structural dimensions of what is happening around you, and don't take things personally. Return to the first step of reading and introspection.

KEY PRINCIPLE:

Develop an antiracist training regime that works with your life and embrace the discomfort that comes with intervening in racist situations. Don't take anything too personally. It's not about you.

HOW CAN WE BUILD THE WORLD WE DESERVE?

Society is not static. Pressure from competing ideas about what is important keeps it in a process of transformation. Some of these ideas are clearly in the foreground of public debate, such as economic development, environmental sustainability, public health, and even reconciliation with Indigenous Peoples. The background is important too, because society is also transforming based on pressures much more difficult to see — structural white supremacy, heteropatriarchy, classism — and resistance to these forms of structural oppression also moves the dial in different directions, though it rarely gets mainstream media or political attention.

In this chapter, we explore controversial everyday things like voting and policing, as well as abstract concepts like the ethics of capitalism. In speaking simultaneously to concrete and abstract concerns that everyone in a liberal democratic society engages with, we aim to highlight some of the stumbling blocks in the way of building a socially just world. People can build the society they deserve through practice. Positive social change can't be achieved like in a video game, where you eventually beat levels one to five and then take on the big villain at the end. People who have amassed power and privilege through accidents of birth are often unwilling to part with that privilege and desperate to argue they have earned these privileges through their grit and hard work.

This isn't new. The British Empire saw itself as a benevolent ruler, "improving" and "developing" the societies within its imperial clutches. The power the British amassed at the expense of those over whom they ruled was understood by defenders of the empire as earned and deserved. Attempts to overthrow the British Empire were rarely successful, and freedom-seeking people in the late nineteenth century and early twentieth century started developing different strategies for defeating empire. One of these strategies was based on making individual British citizens understand that the power and privilege they had was unjust.

Mohandas K. Gandhi was a complicated person in many respects, but he was clear in his thinking that social justice is best served when the oppressor comes to understand that they are oppressing and then chooses not to oppress. Gandhi believed learning the truth about how imperialism privileged British people in unjust and violent ways would ultimately enable them to reject their dominant position and walk away from India as friends rather than be repelled as enemies. This is, at least in a rudimentary way, the basis of the Gandhian method of *satyagraha*, or "truth force," premised on the Jain notion of *ahimsa*, or nonviolence. The British did exit India in 1947, and Gandhi certainly played an important role in making that happen, though the centrality of *satyagraha* tends to overshadow many other forms of resistance that played an enormous role in making India ungovernable for the British.[30] We don't think the British Empire understood itself as being oppressive and then left; such a narrative obscures the millions of South Asians who fought tooth and nail and sacrificed their lives for the cause of national liberation. We do think it's important to learn from Gandhi's method, however, because his tactics certainly did play a big part in educating British people about how they oppressed South Asians and teaching South Asians about how they were stronger than the empire.

Gandhi's vision for India is not the India that exists today. Gandhi imagined an India that was self-sufficient, that turned inward and resuscitated much of what was lost through the colonial encounter. His position exaggerated the level of solidarity among groups within India, and his efforts to create a modern yet traditional nation worked to oppress castes like the Dalits[31] and create the conditions that led to the partition of India and Pakistan along religious lines, something he died feeling was a great failure of independence.

● ● ●

Caste, *noun*
A form of social oppression that developed historically in South Asia and prescribes the kind of work a person must do based on their family of birth. One of the most oppressive forms of social exclusion, caste is maintained over generations through marriage within one's own caste group and occupation. Though outlawed today, it continues to shape South Asian societies and the global diaspora in ways similar to race.

Although Gandhi is presented as the poster boy of Indian independence, individuals alone don't determine the outcome of social transformation. Movements are large and dynamic, which is a great source of optimism. Even though human history cannot be altered through individual actions or commitments, what individuals do with their time on Earth matters a great deal. It's still well worth making the effort to transform our daily lives, because it prepares us all for thinking differently about the world we have and the world we need.

Capitalism Is an Ethic

While individuals by and large do not create history, all people are embedded in structural forms of politics such as imperialism, statehood, capitalism, and more. Focusing attention on the structural operation of power is essential for building the world we deserve. Far too much mainstream attention encourages people to think about social change as a question of individual agency. The long story of human evolution and development is actually a story of community care and solidarity, but considering the last five hundred years of history, there are huge incentives in modern society to reject ethics of care and fairness as mere idealism.

Capitalism is often understood as a science or as something ingrained in human nature rather than as a philosophical and ethical approach to life built around the premise of selfishness and greed leading to ultimate efficiency and productivity. Adam Smith, the person most associated with the rise of capitalism, was a moral philosopher and understood much about how capitalism could be transformative in both positive and negative ways. For example, he wrote that society has a moral obligation to offer educational experiences to children and adults alike because he understood the drudgery of working in factories was inhumane. Our point is not to present Smith favourably, just to say the arrival of capitalism was neither accidental nor uncontested. Excellent histories of capitalism are available to read that explain its gendered dimensions in Europe[32] and its racial dimensions around the world.[33] The idea that human society exists because of competition rather than collaboration is a mistake that valorizes the last five centuries at the expense of human history. It also cleanses capitalism and colonialism of the horrors enacted on billions of people to instead focus on things like the efficiency of the Model T production line.

The ethic of capitalism is not normal, but it has been normalized over hundreds of years and treated as if it is a scientific way of understanding human relations on a large scale. Capitalism's knotted development with other normalized structures like patriarchy and racism works to make concerns of gender, race, and environment invisible. The ideal citizen is seen as a free-thinking, chance-taking, straight white male. His ingenuity is the source of great world events and achievements, like freedom (ever seen *Braveheart?*), incredible medical advancements, even democracy itself. Under an ethic of capitalism, the freedom of the few to play is considered more important than the right of the many to survive — a distortion of values where the desires of white male billionaires to launch themselves into space in penis-shaped rocket ships are considered more important than the toll these adventures take on society through environmental degradation and the social cost of directing billions of dollars to serve narrow personal ambitions rather than collectively using resources for vaccines, drinking water, and much more.

For people to accept this unacceptable situation, institutions needed to be built (poor houses, asylums, schools, residential "schools," prisons) to persuade people to behave as they "ought" to and incarcerate and punish those who deviated, to paraphrase the social theorist Michel Foucault.[34] These institutions that help to control and shape society arose out of the wealth accumulated historically through displacement of women from economies, Indigenous genocide, African slavery, Asian indentureship, unethical and unconscionable experimentation on nonwhite people, and more horrifying shit. Although colonialism has ended in much of the world — at least officially — predominantly brown and Black countries continue to service predominantly white-dominated countries economically. Rather than confront the historical and contemporary causes of this situation today, most white-majority countries prefer an ahistorical shoulder shrug; they believe this is the cost of living in the modern world. In this modern world, it is rational to elect billionaires like Donald Trump to run a powerful state, and taxing the ultra-rich is world-destroying communism rather than prudent public policy.

● ● ●

Carceral system, *noun*
The various institutions in society designed to punish, remove, and change the behaviour of those who deviate from legal and social expectations. Examples include the prison system, criminal justice system, and foster homes.

This stuff might sound abstract, but you can easily see it in your everyday life. Who cleans the toilets and who makes the decisions about wages at your workplace? Why are there so many physicians driving taxis in major Canadian cities while most of the country languishes in medical purgatory? The elites say that privatization and two-tiered health care is the most efficient way to deal with a strained health system because this solution is "market based," when instead the government could change how it recognizes trained doctors, vetting medical schools in countries that send a lot of migrants to Canada in order to bring them directly into the workforce. The inertia of society's privileging of whiteness and capitalism, the embodiments of civilization and freedom, respectively, have normalized the idea that it's just too hard to do things differently.

Defunding Policing, Refunding Society

When people don't do what those with power in society want them to do, police are called upon to exert force until those people conform or are removed from society through the carceral system. We receive recurring what-if questions about policing, especially the idea of defunding the police, from white people, so we would be remiss if we did not say something on the subject here. We encourage readers looking for a deep dive on this issue to read the work of experts on policing and the carceral state.[35]

Omali Yeshitela, chairman of the us-based African People's Socialist Party and prominent leader of the Uhuru ("freedom" in Swahili) movement, explained the situation this way:

You have the emergence in human society of this thing that's called the state. What is the state? The state is this organized bureaucracy. It is the police department. It is the army, the navy. It is the prison system, the courts, and what have you. This is the state — it is a repressive organization. But the state: And gee, well, you know, you've got to have the police 'cause if there were no police look at what you'd be doing to yourselves. You'd be killing each other if there were no police! But the reality is the police become necessary in human society only at that junction in human society when it is split between those who have and those who ain't got.[36]

Yeshitela is absolutely right about the emergence of policing as a means of enforcing law to protect inequalities in society. Children are taught in school that laws are just because they are laws, and those who break laws need to be controlled by society. At some basic level, a society needs to have broad agreement on what its rules are, but simply because something is lawful does not mean it is just. Something can be both lawful and awful, such as residential "schools" or blocking migrants because of their country of origin. Not long ago, groups of white men would try to catch self-emancipated people and drag them back in chains to their "masters," in an enforcement of laws existing at the time. Laws are socially constructed and reflect the values of people with power in any given society.

When activists and scholars talk about defunding the police, they are drawing attention to the incredible amount of resources used to enforce laws that have an irrefutably disproportionate impact on racialized and impoverished people. A better way of keeping society safe is to reallocate funding to important organizations and groups that have been championing progressive causes like housing and universal health care access (in Canada the deep defunding of social programs in the 1990s is still felt today) or in some cases do not yet exist but are needed. To fund police at an exorbitantly high level, governments have cut funding to other vital parts of society that work to keep people safe and secure, including community organizations, mental health and public health organizations, social housing initiatives, and more. In a vicious cycle, the absence of essential health and social services becomes a police issue in the sense that people (especially white people) call the police to deal with any problem they can't or won't solve themselves. In turn, the police point to their inability to deal with a broadening suite of issues and demand larger budgets, which they typically receive. Defunding the police, in the most general sense, is about shifting the priorities of society so the billions of dollars deployed each year to criminalize and incarcerate racialized and poor people can be used instead to help transform society into a fairer and more equitable place.[37]

An understanding of the need for "refunding" society makes clear the police are only one important part of the problem. They are especially visible because they are the point at which state power is physically applied and enforced. Although individual racists are present in the police force, replacing those racist individuals with a greater diversity of police officers does nothing to change the oppressive structure of policing itself, which has been built on generations of enforcing the ethic of capitalism and settler colonialism. (We could say the same of the university and other public institutions.) Don't get us wrong: it is important to identify and remove racists from positions of power, but structural change at the level of society won't come from removing "a few bad apples." Behind the police are masses of policymakers, bureaucrats, politicians of many different levels and jurisdictions, and civil society oversight organizations that usually see themselves as serving the interests of the police rather than holding them accountable to the public.[38]

Our thoughts on this issue are not meant to be representative of social movements engaged in this work — there are a wide range of views about the role of policing in society, and many people advocate for the full dismantling of carceral systems and the creation of better alternatives. Ardath Whynacht's book *Insurgent Love* explains the importance of alternatives to the carceral system even when a person's transgressions are especially heinous.[39] In the southern Mexican state of Chiapas, for example, the Zapatistas have no tolerance for policing because they recognize that police have been prime perpetrators of violence against Indigenous people. Part of the brilliance of defunding the police as a policy measure is it forces people more generally to consider the ways they are implicated in a lawful but awful system that sustains colonial-era inequalities through the crude use of state violence.

• • •

Settler colonialism, *noun*
A form of colonialism where settlers from the colonizing power seek to replace the Indigenous population through genocide and forced assimilation while securing possession of territory. It is best understood as a form of colonialism where the settler never leaves.

Voting

Politics is not limited to a ballot box, but if you watch mainstream news you might think elections and parliaments are the be-all and end-all of political life. A common gripe among politicians and political analysts is the electorate has become apathetic about voting. But the absurd statement "If you don't vote, you don't get to have an opinion" works to discourage meaningful political action, reducing it to marking an "x" next to some person's name once every four or five years. It's not really your fault if you feel apathetic about voting — that problem rests with Canada's truly uninspiring system of representative democracy. During SSFWQ we are often asked for our opinions on voting and racial justice. In a nutshell, no vote is going to bring about racial justice. Electoral systems modelled after European semifeudal political systems designed to reward the same kinds of political thinking, couched in moderately different rhetoric, do not really provide democratic choice.

● ● ●

Representative democracy, *noun*

A form of democracy in which a person is elected to represent the political interests of a number of people, called constituents. It differs from direct democracy, which is a system in which all individuals represent themselves and their interests. There are many forms of representative democracy. In Canada most elections are determined by the first-past-the-post model, in which the candidate in a given geographic area (called a riding) that wins the greatest number of votes is tasked with representing the entire area. Other systems of representative democracy include proportional representation, where voters choose a political party and the proportion of votes for each party is mapped onto how many seats that party receives.

The question of whether to vote is a personal decision, but both of us vote whenever asked. In our view voting is something you can do in five to ten minutes (most of the time), and it is about choosing who you are going to be fighting rather than who you are going to be supporting. Countries with first-past-the-post electoral systems, such as Canada, do not truly have a "positive" vote, meaning a system in which a voter can confidently believe their vote goes to work for them. This type of electoral system is based on delivering majority support in any given riding to whoever wins the most votes, even if that might represent only 25 percent of people who voted. All that matters is who gets "past the post" first, and whoever that is becomes tasked with representing everyone in their geographic riding. This system would make more sense if a riding were like a village where everyone knew one another and could come together to talk to their member of parliament regularly and advise them on what kind of policies needed to take form. But it's not the year 1215, and the electoral system could use an overhaul.

There are many alternative voting systems, including the single-transferrable vote (where you rank candidates, and if your top choice has no chance of winning, your vote transfers to your second choice and so on) and different forms of proportional representation that are not even always tied to geography. But every serious effort to engage in electoral reform (at least three serious attempts have been at the provincial and federal levels in the last twenty years) has been sabotaged by one of the two big parties that have ruled Canada since Confederation, because these two parties benefit enormously from the current unfair electoral system.

Canadian electors have a "negative" vote in that they can try to vote *against* the worst-case scenario in their riding. Partisans (people who are loyal to a party) decry this kind of strategic voting as the reason why smaller parties cannot get a foot in the door, but we find that argument unpersuasive because voting "positively" for a smaller party means supporting a party with no chance of winning in the vain hope that thousands of other people are doing the same thing. If someone wants to vote for the Greens or an independent candidate in a riding with a close race between the NDP and the Conservatives, for example, they are free to do so, but there's no hope of their "positive" vote playing a role beyond garnering a buck or two for the party of their choice. Canada has had more than 150 years of first-past-the-post electoral practice and the outcome at the federal level has always been a Liberal or Conservative government. Without electoral reform, it's difficult to see how the genuine will of electors can be translated into Parliament.

We cannot reduce politics to voting. Voting is important, but not that important. In the hierarchy of political involvement, voting should be near the bottom of your list, above signing a petition but below participating in a public demonstration or rally. But still *do* the things on the bottom of your list, just like you wash dishes or fold the laundry. Having organized against the Harper Conservatives and the Trudeau Liberals, we know they require different strategies because of the different kinds of ideological approaches they subscribe to. But regardless of who has been governing in recent decades, any progress made towards a better society has mainly come about because people and social movements forced the issue. Electoral politics is merely the tip of the political iceberg — voters can choose who they will inevitably have to fight, and that's still an important choice. Like one of our favourite community newspapers wrote over a decade ago, vote, but vote without faith.[40]

Building Alternatives through Practice

You don't need to have the alternatives figured out before engaging in the work of cultivating new forms of relations. But a commonly deployed conservative scare tactic says you do, in order to discourage people from experimenting with differences. The fear of "letting in too many Asians" was a defining characteristic of Canadian immigration history, for example, and society lives with the legacy of this thinking. Anti-Asian hate crimes in Canada — at least those people bothered to report — increased by 300 percent from 2019 to 2020, according to Statistics Canada.[41] In the city of Vancouver in this same period, hate crimes against Asian people increased by 717 percent, according to police statistics.[42] Political terminology from the not-too-distant 1990s included "Asian invasions," used to describe immigration from Hong Kong in particular, and more recently this has played out in criticisms of how Asian people live in "monster homes," especially in British Columbia. At the root of these forms of racism is a dominant Eurocentric culture that has been challenged by the presence of noticeable numbers of people from non-European cultures. Sure, some Asian immigrants live in larger homes if they can afford it, in part to take care of their intergenerational families. This defies market conceptions of things like childcare because for many Asians in Canada, cultural continuity across generations happens by maintaining strong bonds with great-grandparents, grandparents, and children. This helps protect the integrity of languages, which are bastions of knowledge and also an audible nonconformity that often triggers white aggression, against Asian elders in particular.

There are practical everyday ways to build alternatives even within structures that are oppressive, and the family structure is a great starting point. It might mean working to recognize that the nuclear family, or the Western conception of a married couple with 2.5 kids in daycare, is not the only or best way to organize society. The accusation of "overcrowding" in homes has been levelled against nonwhite families as an excuse for the state to incarcerate children, taking them out of their families, placing them in foster care, and breaking bonds of kinship that have had tremendous value in Indigenous Nations and communities, as well as for many people of African and Asian ancestry.

The work of normalizing alternatives does not have to be radical. We discussed the virtues of interfering in the inertia of structural forms of oppression — one easy way we have found to do this is at a barbecue. Picture, if you will, a group of guys standing around the grill, giving each other advice about when to turn over whatever object happens to be on there. They get to talking about hockey or basketball or another sport. When you speak on the subject, make mention of your favourite trans athlete without fixating on their identity; just talk about them as you would any other athlete. Or mention the Punjabi-language broadcasting of hockey on the West Coast that offers an alternative to the open racism of Hockey Night in Canada. Here's a hypothetical example to show you what it might look like, at least if you're a cis male BBQ goer:

DAVE: Well, Chuck, I think it's about time to turn that flank of animal flesh over.

CHUCK: Not a chance, Dave. Believe me, I'm the king of this castle. Read the apron. [chuckles]

JEFF: Did anyone catch the game last night?

DAVE: I missed it because the wife made me go get balloons for the birthday party tomorrow. But I caught the high-light reels after.

YOU: I watched Hockey Night in Canada in Punjabi. They had some really good analysis of the footage. You should check it out!

DAVE: You all play hockey in India?

YOU: I don't know, never been to India. There's a ton of people of Indian ancestry in Canada who love hockey though.

It takes a little bit of preparation, of course. If you're going to a BBQ, a gendered division of attendees might emerge and gendered topics of conversation might come up. So you prepare a few talking points ahead of time, but respect the flow of the conversation as best you can.

In the above conversation (which we have encountered dozens of times), there are lots of things you could choose to take issue with. The objectification of women via reducing a person's identity to her relationship to her husband ("the wife"), for example, could be the basis of your intervention instead. But effective communication means picking one thing at a time, because if you try to deconstruct the problematic nature of people's subconsciously ingrained structural forms of oppression, you'll probably wind up sounding like a conde-scending jerk as described in Chapter 5. By respecting the intent and flow of the unfolding conversation and not trying to tell people they are wrong to assume Indians don't play hockey or to reduce a woman's identity to her relationship to a man, or whatever, you can still engage in meaningful conversations that plant seeds for future consideration. People understand things better when they make connections and draw conclusions themselves rather than being told by someone else.

Finally, building the world we deserve means embracing the role of conflict in our lives. Most people despise conflict — it makes them feel heavy in their stomachs, or they want to run and hide. But conflict doesn't have to be a bad thing. Only through conflict can people tethered to a strong sense of what is "normal" start to think differently. Most of the things impacting your everyday life and the quality of life for those around you happen at the individual level. Individuals can't always impact structure, at least not all the time. But you can start to build. As Ottawa-based educator and podcaster Adrienne Coddett once said, "Even a washing machine needs an agitator, otherwise we're just sitting in dirty water."

K E Y   P R I N C I P L E :

Individuals alone do not transform society, because oppression is structural. But by thinking and acting critically in the everyday, you can build alternatives over the long term. Remember, people are more comfortable thinking about different ideas when they are not overwhelmed with information and analysis all at once.

THE RACE CARD

If we had a dollar for every time we've been accused of "playing the race card," we would give up our day jobs and learn how to play cards. Race is not a card game though; it never was, and we can't imagine how it ever could be. If you unpack the meaning underlying the charge of "playing the race card" or the "gender card" or the "queer card" and so forth, you find a thinly veiled attempt to reduce the complexity and realities of someone's life to the whims of a leisurely pastime. Think about what it means to suggest that race is a card being played — life is a game and everyone is sitting around together shuffling cards. But while some people are playing cards, others are serving the drinks and snacks, and still others are manufacturing cards they will never have time to play with. Only people who have not lived the daily indignities, aggressions, invalidations, and violence of structural white supremacy could possibly even think to reduce this experience to a casual game of cards.

In presenting a top ten list of frequently asked white questions along with some basic thoughts on these subjects, we hope to have sparked interest in readers to do their own work to educate themselves and perhaps even engage in antiracist organizing of their own. We began the book by discussing structural racism itself by explaining why it's not possible to be racist against white people. Building on this foundation, Chapter 2 picked up on some of the anxious questions white people have related to general fears about what justice-seeking movements, including Indigenous sovereignty and reparations for slavery and colonialism, mean for their quality of life. We also offered notes on how to receive constructive criticism in a good way. Chapter 3 connected racism to other forms of structural oppression and introduced the important concept of intersectionality, which we returned to throughout the book. Chapter 4 spoke to family life, including raising antiracist children and separating race from culture. In Chapter 5 we picked up the theme of how to communicate progressive political ideas in a way that does not condescend or capitulate to the inertia of the status quo, which in our estimation has a conservative-liberal resting face. Chapter 6 tackled the popular topics of cultural appropriation and cancel culture, and Chapter 7 revisited intersectionality through a discussion of equity, diversity, inclusion, and accessibility. In Chapter 8 we explored how white people can be involved in antiracist work without centring themselves, and we built on this discussion in Chapter 9 by outlining strategies for bringing antiracism into your everyday lives by using racial privilege strategically. Finally, in Chapter 10 we returned to the theme of collective liberation by exploring how people can build the world they deserve over time, in big and small ways, rather than just going along with the oppressive world they have inherited.

Structural white supremacy, like other forms of structural privilege and oppression, needs to be carefully and systematically dismantled because it is in everyone's best interest for it to go away. We believe white people, like all people, are overwhelmingly motivated by a strong desire to be good and ethical and just need a little extra help to see things not immediately in their field of vision. Just as men need a little help to understand how heteropatriarchy impacts their lives and the lives of the women and gender-nonconforming people around them, white people equipped with the basic tools and foundations upon which to begin unlearning the implicit lessons of structural white supremacy will ultimately educate themselves and others. There is no potential for an equitable society until people are able to have difficult conversations with one another and encourage them rather than run away and hide behind whatever rules or procedures might be in place to silence discussions of this nature.

Part of refusing to play cards with race is taking the experience of whiteness seriously. Whiteness is a lens through which people come to understand the world, and it is the most powerful lens through which perceptions of what is "normal" or "beautiful" or "desirable" are reflected in modern nation-states. In this sense, we engaged in two simultaneous projects in this book.

The first was to provide accessible entry points for white people to develop some of the basic tools needed to chip away at the powerful forces in society that encourage them to avoid thinking about race. To achieve this, we aimed to be informative but somewhat lighthearted. We sought to valorize discomfort and normalize important, cringey conversations around dinner tables, in reading groups, and with children, so white people can build up the resilience needed to have discussions about race without getting defensive or dismissive. We do not want to have situations like the youth conference described in the introduction, where nonwhite kids are treated like texts for white kids to learn from while the ensuing conflict could be driving others into the fold of white nationalism rather than tackling the issue in a supportive environment. We would prefer that white people develop some baseline understanding of these issues first using texts like FAWQ and others (see our recommended reading list at the end of the book), so conversations with their nonwhite friends and family are of a higher quality and more beneficial for everyone.

The recurring problem of white people confusing structural racism for an indictment of themselves as racists speaks to the fundamental problem of confusing agents and structures, or the individual case for the general context. In many ways, this single sociological point is at the root of everything we have written about in this book — white fragility and anxieties about race come from a socialized knee-jerk reaction to think the best way to live in a free and democratic society is to treat everyone the same. This liberal elixir is intoxicating, because it has allowed for breakthroughs that make it seem as though society is fundamentally transformed. For example, the appointment of Jody Wilson-Raybould as justice minister, the first Indigenous woman in Canada to hold the position, was important but totally insufficient to bring about the legal transformations needed to address the structural white supremacy impacting how the Canadian state interacts with Indigenous people.

When a white person tells us they are worried their son is not going to be able to find work when he grows up because of equity-based hiring practices, we do not dismiss that concern as a "race card" either. Concern for children is one of the most universal human experiences, and it can be a powerful way to think about building horizontal solidarities. We hope our efforts to honestly think through frequently asked white questions will be helpful to white people. We encourage them to think harder and longer about racial justice so they do not consciously or subconsciously accuse someone of playing cards with race just because the substance of that person's argument triggers an emotional feeling. One of the great ironies of modern society is people act as if they already live in a merit-based world yet balk at any measures to actually make structural changes that could make equity part of everyone's lived experience.

We hope FAWQ's small contribution can help build up racial resilience as a counterpoint to white fragility as well as "white pride" and other forms of toxic nationalism. Racial resilience helps to have these conversations, so the kinds of issues in this book are really intended to be the foundation upon which much more challenging and thoughtful conversations can be built. Readers of the book must do that work themselves; this is a support to get you started or help you along the way.

Finally, our second and not-so-covert objective in this book is to create resources for well-intentioned white people that also make life easier for exhausted racialized people everywhere. Our musings on the ten important themes covered in each chapter are not the definitive "social justice" or even "racialized" perspective on these issues. Instead, what we hope we have offered is enough of a starting point for white readers in terms of common points of concern so they won't turn to the nonwhite people in their lives without having done a little homework first. If you are a nonwhite person reading this book, we hope that being able to prescribe FAWQ or flip someone the link to the free SSFWQ YouTube series can save you enough time and energy to maybe pick up a real deck of cards and enjoy your evening.

TOP TEN PRINCIPLES FOR THINKING ABOUT RACIAL POLITICS AS A WHITE PERSON

1   White people experience many forms of intersecting oppression, but they cannot experience racism because we live in a world structured by white supremacy.

2   The process of building alternatives requires courage and humility to make good mistakes and draw meaningful lessons from those mistakes so the generosity of those who help you to learn is not squandered.

3   Racism is one especially odious form of structural oppression that intersects with other forms of structural oppression, such as classism and misogyny. Race is not

biologically real, but the implications of who counts as fully human, and the material consequences of that, certainly are.

4   Bringing antiracism into family life is essential and can be done through role modelling, building stronger mechanisms of communication between loved ones, and preparing kids to engage the world as it is.

5   When involved in an argument or disagreement, look for the root causes and underlying anxieties leading a person to hold discriminatory views. Empathy and care can be more effective than condescension and disbelief, especially in terms of modelling better behaviour for the witnessing silent majority.

6   Other people's cultures aren't your all-you-can-eat buffet. When oppressed and marginalized people object to the way they are depicted in public, try to consider in good faith their reasons for doing so. Respectful and sincere cultural appreciation, learning, and exchange is possible, necessary, and beautiful, but not on terms set by white supremacy, heteronormativity, settler colonialism, and capitalism.

7   Beware of binary thinking and how thinking in "black and white" terms compels you to sacrifice context. Claim all of who you are and use the privileges you have for positive social change.

8 If you are a white person looking to be involved in antiracist work, don't try to be a saviour, don't wallow in penitence, and most definitely do not turn it into a grift. Find ways to turn your unearned privilege into a tool to dismantle white supremacy and prioritize educating and organizing other white people as part of a wider struggle for collective liberation.

9 Develop an antiracist training regime that works with your life and embrace the discomfort that comes with intervening in racist situations. Don't take anything too personally. It's not about you.

10 Individuals alone do not transform society, because oppression is structural. But by thinking and acting critically in the everyday, you can build alternatives over the long term. Remember, people are more comfortable thinking about different ideas when they are not overwhelmed with information and analysis all at once.

NOTES

1   Rashawn Ray and Alexandra Gibbons, "Why Are States Banning Critical Race Theory?" *FixGov* (blog), November 21, 2021. brookings.edu/blog/ fixgov/2021/07/02/why-are-states-banning-critical-race-theory.

2   Angela Saini, *Superior: The Return of Race Science* (Boston: Beacon Press, 2019).

3   Peter Linebaugh and Marcus Rediker, *The Many-Headed Hydra: Sailors, Slaves, Commoners, and the Hidden History of the Revolutionary Atlantic* (Boston: Beacon Press, 2000); Silvia Federici, *Caliban and the Witch: Women, the Body and Primitive Accumulation* (New York: Autonomedia, 2003).

4   Charles W. Mills, *The Racial Contract* (Ithaca: Cornell University Press, 1997).

5   David R. Roediger, *The Wages of Whiteness: Race and the Making of the American Working Class*, rev. ed (London: Verso, 2007).

6   Scot Wortley, *Halifax, Nova Scotia: Street Checks Report* (Halifax: NS Human Rights Commission, 2019). humanrights.novascotia.ca/sites/default/ files/editor-uploads/halifax_street_checks_report_march_2019_0.pdf.

7   Roediger, *Wages of Whiteness*.

8   For a detailed explanation of sovereignty with reading lists, discussion questions, and exercises, see Ajay Parasram, "Sovereignty beyond Eurocentricity," in *Showing Theory to Know Theory: Understanding Social Science Concepts through Illustrative Vignettes*, eds. P. Ballamingie and D. Szanto (Ottawa: Showing Theory Press). https://doi.org/10.22215/sktk/pa44.

9   Glen Sean Coulthard, *Red Skin White Masks: Rejecting the Colonial Politics of Recognition* (Minneapolis: University of Minnesota Press, 2014); Dorene

Bernard, "Reconciliation and Environmental Racism in Mi'kma'ki," *Kalfou* 5, 2 (2018). https://doi.org/10.15367/kf.v5i2.214; Leanne Betasamosake Simpson, "The Brilliance of Beaver: Learning from an Anishnaabe World," April 16, 2020, in *Ideas*, audio lecture, 53:59, cbc.ca/player/play/1725600323622; M'sit No'kmaq et al., "'Awakening the Sleeping Giant': Re-Indigenization Principles for Transforming Biodiversity Conservation in Canada and Beyond," *Facets* 6 (2021). https://doi.org/10.1139/facets-2020-0083.

10 Shashi Tharoor, "Britain Does Owe Reparations," Oxford Union Debate, July 14, 2015, YouTube video, 15:28, youtube.com/watch?v=f7CW7S0zxv4; see also Shashi Tharoor, *Inglorious Empire: What the British Did to India* (London: Hurst, 2017).

11 C.L.R. James, *The Black Jacobins: Toussaint L'Ouverture and The San Domingo Revolution* (New York: Vintage Books, 1968[1938]).

12 Dariusz Dziewanski, "Fight Violence with More Social Spending, Not More Police," *Policy Options*, September 9, 2020. policyoptions.irpp.org/magazines/september-2020/fight-violence-with-more-social-spending-not-more-police.

13 Combahee River Collective, *The Combahee River Collective Statement*, April 1977, historyisaweapon.com/defcon1/combrivercoll.html.

14 Kimberlé Crenshaw, "Demarginalizing the Intersection of Race and Sex: A Black Feminist Critique of Antidiscrimination Doctrine, Feminist Theory and Antiracist Policies," *University of Chicago Legal Forum* 1989, 1 (1989).

15 Saini, *Superior*.

16 Wortley, *Street Checks Report*.

17 Michael Halpin, "Incels Are Surprisingly Diverse but United by Hate," *The Conversation*, July 7, 2021. theconversation.com/incels-are-surprisingly-diverse-but-united-by-hate-163414.

18 Paul Buhle and Nicole Schulman, eds., *Wobblies!: A Graphic History of the Industrial Workers of the World* (London: Verso, 2005); Peter Cole, David

Struthers, and Kenyon Zimmer, eds., *Wobblies of the World: A Global History of the IWW* (London: Pluto Press, 2017).

19 George Lipsitz, *The Possessive Investment in Whiteness: How White People Profit from Identity Politics*, 20th anniversary ed. (Philadelphia: Temple University Press, 2018).

20 Lorenzo Veracini, *Settler Colonialism: A Theoretical Overview* (New York: Palgrave, 2010).

21 Harsha Walia, *Undoing Border Imperialism* (Oakland: AK Press, 2014); Harsha Walia, *Border and Rule* (Halifax: Fernwood Publishing, 2021).

22 Ajay Parasram and Nissim Mannathukkaren, "Imperial Afterlives: Citizenship and Race/Caste Fragility in Canada and India," *Citizenship Studies* (2021). https://doi.org/10.1080/13621025.2021.1984494.

23 Corey Snelgrove, Rita Dhamoon, and Jeff Corntassel, "Unsettling Settler Colonial Studies: The Discourse and Politics of Settlers, and Solidarity with Indigenous Nations," *Decolonization: Indigeneity, Education & Society* 3, 2 (2014).

24 Chris Dixon, *Another Politics: Talking across Today's Transformative Movements* (Berkeley: University of California Press, 2014).

25 Incite! Women of Color Against Violence, *The Revolution Will Not Be Funded: Beyond the Non-Profit Industrial Complex* (Cambridge: South End Press, 2007).

26 This list is not comprehensive, because, gladly, it's an issue many continue to write on. In no particular order: Crystal M. Fleming, *How to Be Less Stupid about Race* (Boston: Beacon Press, 2018); Ijeoma Oluo, *So You Want to Talk about Race* (New York: Seal Press, 2018); Ibram X. Kendi, *How to Be an Anti-Racist* (New York: One World, Penguin Random House, 2019); Layla F. Saad, *Me and White Supremacy: Combat Racism, Change the World, and Become a Good Ancestor* (Naperville: Sourcebooks, 2020); Fern L. Johnson and Marlene G. Fine, *Let's Talk Race: A Guide for White People* (Gabriola Island: New Society, 2021).

27   W.E.B. Dubois, *The Souls of Black Folks* (Chicago: A.C. McClurg, 1903); Frantz Fanon, *Black Skin White Masks*, trans. Richard Philcox (New York: Grove Press, 2008); Sherene Razack, *Looking Whiteness in the Eye: Gender, Race, and Culture in Courtrooms and Classrooms* (Toronto: University of Toronto Press, 1998); Sunera Thobani, *Exalted Subjects: Studies in the Making of Race and Nation in Canada* (Toronto: University of Toronto Press, 2007); Carol Anderson, *White Rage: The Unspoken Truth about the Racial Divide* (New York: Bloomsbury, 2016); El Jones, "Sydney Crosby Should Have Done Better," *Vice*, September 26, 2017. vice.com/en/article/kz734y/sidney-crosby-should-have-done-better; Gurminder K. Bhambra, "Brexit, Trump, and 'Methodological Whiteness': On the Misrecognition of Race and Class," *British Journal of Sociology* 68 (2017). https://doi.org/10.1111/1468-4446.12317; Errol Henderson, "Hidden in Plain Sight: Racism in International Relations Theory," *Cambridge Review of International Affairs* 26, 1 (2013). https://doi.org/10.1080/09557571.2012.710585.

28   Louise, how *could* you?

29   Jacques Rancière, Davide Panagia, and Rachel Bowlby, "Ten Theses on Politics," *Theory & Event* 5, 3 (2001) https://doi.org/10.1353/tae.2001.0028.

30   Maia Ramnath, *Decolonizing Anarchism: An Antiauthoritarian History of India's Liberation Struggle* (Oakland: AK Press, 2011); Arundhati Roy, *The Doctor and the Saint: Caste, Race, and the Annihilation of Caste, the Debate Between B.R. Ambedkar and M.K. Gandhi* (Chicago: Haymarket, 2017).

31   The caste system in India is a precolonial and rigid form of social oppression that divides people by family of birth, dictating what kinds of labour and socialization they can and cannot do. Though banned in India due to the legal efforts of B.R. Ambedkar, it persists. Ambedkar and Gandhi did not see eye to eye on key reforms needed to ensure the active participation of lower-caste Indians in what would become postcolonial India. For more details, readers can consult Chinnaiah Jangam, *Dalits and the Making of Modern India* (Delhi: Oxford University Press, 2017). For more on the tensions between Gandhi and Ambedkar, see Arundhati Roy, *The Doctor and the Saint*.

32   Federici, *Caliban and the Witch*.

33 Cedric Robinson, *Black Marxism: The Making of the Black Radical Tradition* (London: Zed Press, 1983); Coulthard, *Red Skin, White Masks*; Eric Williams, *Capitalism and Slavery* (London: Andre Deutsch, 1944)

34 Michel Foucault, *Security, Territory, Population: Lectures at the College de France*, trans. Graham Burchell (New York: Palgrave, 2009).

35 Angela Davis, *Abolition Democracy: Beyond Empire, Prisons, and Torture* (New York: Seven Stories Press, 2005); Jordan T. Camp and Christina Heatherton, eds., *Policing the Planet: Why the Policing Crisis Led to Black Lives Matter* (London: Verso, 2016); Robin Maynard, *Policing Black Lives: State Violence in Canada from Slavery to the Present* (Halifax: Fernwood Publishing, 2017); Andrew Crosby and Jeffrey Monaghan, *Policing Indigenous Movements: Dissent and the Security State* (Halifax: Fernwood Publishing, 2018); Desmond Cole, *The Skin We're In: A Year of Black Resistance and Power* (Toronto: DoubleDay Canada, 2020); El Jones, *Abolitionist Intimacies* (Halifax: Fernwood Publishing, 2022); Ardath Whynacht, *Insurgent Love: Abolition and Domestic Homocide* (Halifax: Fernwood Publishing, 2021); Alex S. Vitale, *The End of Policing*, updated paperback ed. (New York: Verso, 2021).

36 This excerpt of a speech by Chairman Omali Yeshitela appears at the beginning of Dead Prez's song "Police State" from the 2000 album *Let's Get Free*.

37 Patricia Conor, Sophie Carrière, Suzanne Amey, Sharon Marcellus, and Julie Sauvé, *Police Resources in Canada, 2019* (Ottawa: Statistics Canada, 2020). www150.statcan.gc.ca/n1/pub/85-002-x/2020001/article/00015-eng.htm.

38 Board of the Police Commissioner's Subcommittee to Define Defunding Police, *Defunding the Police: Defining the Way Forward for HRM.* halifax.ca/sites/default/files/documents/city-hall/boards-committees-commissions/220117bopc1021.pdf.

39 Whynacht, *Insurgent Love*.

40 The Leveller Editorial Board, "Voting without Faith," *The Leveller*, April 19, 2011. leveller.ca/2011/04/voting-without-faith.

41 Jing Hui Wang and Greg Moreau, "Police-Reported Hate Crime in Canada, 2020," *Statistics Canada*. www150.statcan.gc.ca/n1/pub/85-002-x/2022001/ article/00005-eng.htm.

42 Vancouver Police Department, *Year-End 2020 Year-to-Date Key Performance Indicators Report*, February 3, 2021. vancouverpoliceboard.ca/police/police-board/agenda/2021/0218/5-1-2102P01-Year-end-2020-KPI-Report.pdf.

GLOSSARY

Agents and structures: Society is composed of agents, or individuals, who are part of many kinds of structures, or institutions. A structure can refer to a place, like a parliament, or it can refer to a form of social power, such as heterosexuality. Agents are embedded within structures in any given society, and structures shape people's understanding of what is "normal." At the same time, structures can shift and transform as a result of pressure exerted by agents within them.

Cancel culture: A term commonly used to describe the feeling that leftists or people who identify with progressive politics seek to deplatform and silence anyone who uses harmful and outdated words or ideas. It is popularly used in defences of freedom of speech with no expectation of accuracy or accountability.

Capitalism: An economic system and ideology based on the production of commodities for sale on the market in pursuit of profit. Under this system, workers must sell their labour in exchange for a wage to survive.

Carceral system: The various institutions in society designed to punish, remove, and change the behaviour of those who deviate from legal and social expectations. Examples include the prison system, criminal justice system, and foster homes.

Caste: A form of social oppression that developed historically in South Asia and prescribes the kind of work a person must do based on their family of birth. One of the most oppressive forms of social exclusion, caste is maintained over generations through marriage within one's own caste group and occupation. Though outlawed today, it continues to shape South Asian societies and the global diaspora in ways similar to race.

Cis: A term indicating that a person's assigned sex at birth matches their gender identity. Often used as an opposite to "trans."

Collective liberation: Freedom for all, understood in the sense that no one is really free until everyone is, and one group's liberation cannot come at the cost of another's. It also embodies the notion that each struggle against oppression and exploitation is part of a much bigger constellation of freedom struggles.

Colonialism: The process of one people establishing control over another people and their territory with the aim of securing enduring relations of exploitation.

Constructive criticism: A respectful way of giving and receiving feedback motivated by a genuine desire to help the receiver deepen their knowledge and understanding of an issue. Both the receiver and offerer should be ready, calm, and interested for it to be successful.

Critical race theory: A term used by conservative politicians and media darlings to describe interdisciplinary scholarship that approaches the social construction of race as a central issue in modern society. The intent is to discredit the substance of the research and dismiss serious engagements of race in public policy.

Cultural appropriation: The use and abuse of a group's cultural practices by someone from outside that group.

Culture: The shared conceptual framework and corresponding material practices belonging to a group of people who understand themselves as a distinct collective.

Diaspora: A dispersed population of people who share a common place of origin. For example, a sizeable Trinidadian diaspora lives in the Greater Toronto Area.

Eugenics: A pseudoscientific belief system that falsely asserts specific abilities are heritable and so possible to cultivate in or eliminate from society through the selective breeding, sterilization, and culling of people.

Exploitation: The act of living off someone else's labour.

Fascism: A form of revolutionary populist ultranationalism characterized by an obsession with community decline, humiliation, and victimhood and a striving for community rebirth through the purging of internal enemies and external expansion. It is illiberal, antidemocratic, and violent.

Heterosexism: An oppressive social relation based on the misconception that only two genders exist (men and women) and that these genders naturally have distinct and complementary social roles. In this view, the only legitimate intimate relationships are between cis men and women, with all others considered aberrations.

Identity politics: A term coined in the 1970s by the Combahee River Collective, a group of Black, lesbian, radical feminists in the United States, out of a conviction that "the most profound and potentially most radical politics come directly out of our own identity, as opposed to working to end somebody else's oppression."

Incel: This term, meaning "involuntary celibate," was originally coined by a woman but has since been adopted by men (of many racial backgrounds) and used to describe an online and transnational community that peddles misogyny based on a belief that women are denying them sex.

Imperialism: The process of one people expanding their power to rule over other peoples and places. It involves the extension of economic, political, and social domination of one group over another using tools ranging from diplomacy to military force.

Intersectionality: Coined by Kimberlé Crenshaw, this term refers to the overlapping nature of social identity categories, such as race, class, gender, sexuality, age, and ability, and how they work together to sustain structured social relations of privilege and oppression.

Marginalized: Excluded from power, resources, and decision-making in society. Certain groups in society are systematically excluded, in opposition to mainstream or dominant groups.

Microaggressions: Small, everyday incidents where a person's lived experience is trivialized, denied, or made light of through reminders that the person is not part of the dominant group in some way (e.g., not white, not hetero, not male). Racial microaggressions may take the form of constant and effusive remarks about a Black person's hair or the expression of a strong opinion about the hijab without much knowledge about it.

Nibling: A gender-neutral alternative to "niece" and "nephew."

Not-for-profit industrial complex: The array of nonprofit, nongovernmental organizations that claim to address a variety of social justice issues but whose existence is tied to the perpetuation of the problem they claim to confront. This system can often function, intentionally and not, to inhibit rather than empower struggles for social change by guarding access to scarce resources, expertise, and political legitimacy.

Oppression: A collective social phenomenon involving the debasement of a group of people by another group that aims to maintain structured inequality, with tangible, lived, and material benefits for the oppressors and tangible, lived, and material costs for the oppressed.

Patriarchy: Literally "rule of the father," it is a form of oppressive social organization in which men hold power, dominate roles of political or economic leadership, exert moral authority, and exercise disproportionate privilege and control of property.

Populism: An approach to politics that emphasizes the interests of "the people" over those of the elites who exercise control in society. It can take the form of right-wing populism, as seen with former US president Donald Trump and Canadian politicians Maxime Bernier and Pierre Poilievre, or left-wing populism, as exemplified by the late Venezuelan president Hugo Chavez.

Positionality: A way of understanding the importance of one's lived experience and how it affects how one moves through the world. It explains how people may not immediately notice or understand things that are everyday experiences for others.

Power: The ability to exert force or control over others, to exercise one's will regardless of opposition or resistance. Power is not a thing a person has or doesn't have; it is a relationship through which force is exerted in the world and on us.

Race: An identity category of immense social importance but no biological or genetic basis, with which people are categorized based on mainly observable physical characteristics. No evidence exists to substantiate racial groupings, and the scientific consensus is that there is one human species, *Homo sapiens*. Among those who see race as a legitimate way to categorize different human populations, there is no agreement about how many races exist or what clearly and empirically distinguishes them from each other. The concept of race has been used over the last five hundred years as a way to organize and rationalize the theft of independence, territory, labour, resources, and wealth from some groups of people by others. It has also played a central role in some of the worst atrocities in human history.

Racial resilience: The outcome of learning about race as a structure and how it influences present-day institutions, society, and people. Presented as a remedy for white fragility (though it can also address racial fragility experienced by nonwhite people), racial resilience creates a strong basis on which to have serious conversations about race.

Racialized: Categorized and integrated into society's racial hierarchy based on one's perceived race. The implication is that something is being done to racialize a person; they do not naturally exist in a state of "race." Whiteness is a racial identity as well, but because it is at the top of the racial hierarchy people who are white or white-passing rarely understand themselves in racial terms.

Racism: A system of oppressive social relations rooted in the false belief that humanity can be divided into distinct and unequal groups based on arbitrary observable characteristics such as skin colour, with implications for who counts as fully human and who does not.

Representative democracy: A form of democracy in which a person is elected to represent the political interests of a number of people, called constituents. It differs from direct democracy, which is a system in which all individuals represent themselves and their interests. There are many forms of representative democracy. In Canada most elections are determined by the first-past-the-post model, in which the candidate in a given geographic area (called a riding) that wins the greatest number of votes is tasked with representing the entire area. Other systems of representative democracy include proportional representation, where voters choose a political party and the proportion of votes for each party is mapped onto how many seats that party receives.

Respectability politics: A form of political gatekeeping that demands people's struggles for social justice and social change conform to the norms and values of dominant society. This insistence on abiding by prevailing standards of civility disciplines and limits liberation struggles.

Ruling class: The strata of individuals in a society who exercise the greatest power over others. Under capitalism the owners of the means of production make up the ruling class.

Settler colonialism: A form of colonialism where settlers from the colonizing power seek to replace the Indigenous population through genocide and forced assimilation while securing possession of territory. It is best understood as a form of colonialism where the settler never leaves.

Social capital: The resources a person has access to as a result of the social networks of which they are a part.

Social justice warrior: A pejorative term used to describe people who advocate for a more just world through a variety of different ways. In using a catch-all term like this to describe a wide variety of progressive movements, those who are opposed to changing society seek to dismiss the substance of movements without having to engage them meaningfully.

Solidarity: A relationship of mutual aid and support formed through political struggle seeking to challenge forms of oppression.

Sovereignty: A country's claim of total rule over the territories it understands to be within its borders. This formulation is the most common today, coming to prominence in the age of empire and colonialism. There are many other ways to think about sovereignty grounded in land and history across the world, especially in Canada where Indigenous Nations and communities have exercised sovereignty based on principles like reciprocity, solidarity, and responsibility rather than ownership and domination.

Unconscious bias: The false notion that oppression in society emerges from the biases, assumptions, preferences, and prejudices each person carries around inside their heads. From this perspective, forms of oppression like racism and sexism can only be fixed by by having individuals work on themselves to recognize these biases and minimize their impact on decision-making. It entirely sidelines how oppression and exploitation intertwine, how they are entrenched in dominant social institutions, and how they organize social relations.

White supremacy: The belief that white people not only constitute a distinct people in racial and ethnic terms but are superior to nonwhite people. Institutions and states can be white supremacist based on foundational, historical structures that continue to exist today, even if they are not explicitly run by white supremacists.

White nationalism: A political ideology that views white people as a distinct group and calls for the creation of white ethnostates through the expulsion of nonwhite people, often through violent means.

White fragility: The feelings of guilt, anger, and defensiveness experienced and expressed by white people when confronted with situations in which they are forced to understand themselves in racial terms. Popularized by Robin DiAngelo, the term also describes how resources are often redeployed to care for white people's feelings rather than deal with the harm done to nonwhite people.

White solidarity: The unspoken agreement that ideas, cultures, and norms originating in European culture are universally "normal" and all others deviate from this norm. In practice this works to cultivate white fragility by discouraging and derailing conversations that make white people feel uncomfortable about racial politics. Historically, white solidarity has been used to ensure class-based solidarities across racial groups are not sustained by offering small advantages to white workers.

READING LIST

This list has been compiled over two years of SSFWQ episodes. It features books, articles, and other media that have come to our minds while responding to live questions over the course of the series. We continue to add to this list as we host SSFWQ, so it is by no means comprehensive — if you see something missing, feel free to drop into a monthly session and let us know! The SSFWQ series can be found on Fernwood Publishing's YouTube channel.

Peace, Power, and Righteousness: An Indigenous Manifesto by Taiaiake Alfred

Imagined Communities: Reflections on the Origins and Spread of Nationalism by Benedict Anderson

White Rage: The Unspoken Truth of Our Racial Divide by Carol Anderson

The Klu Klux Klan in Canada: A Century of Promoting Racism and Hate in the Peaceable Kingdom by Allan Bartley

"Reconciliation and Environmental Racism in Mi'kma'ki" (tupjournals.temple.edu/ index.php/kalfou/article/view/214) by Dorene Bernard

Global Social Theory website (globalsocialtheory.org) edited by Gurminder K. Bhambra

White Privilege: The Myth of a Post-Racial Society by Kalwant Bhopal

Becoming an Ally: Breaking the Cycle of Oppression in People by Anne Bishop

Policing the Planet: Why the Policing Crisis Led to Black Lives Matter edited by Jordan Camp and Christina Heatherton

The Skin We're In: A Year of Black Resistance and Power by Desmond Cole

The Hanging of Angélique: The Untold Story of Canadian Slavery and the Burning of Old Montréal by Afua Cooper

Black Matters by Afua Cooper

Policing Indigenous Movements: Dissent and the Security State by Andrew Crosby and Jeffrey Monaghan

Red Skin, White Masks: Rejecting the Colonial Politics of Recognition by Glen Coulthard

Women, Race & Class by Angela Davis

Abolition Democracy: Beyond Empire, Prisons, and Torture by Angela Davis

God is Red: A Native View of Religion by Vine Deloria Jr.

Unmooring the Komagata Maru: Charting Colonial Trajectories edited by Rita Kaur Dhamoon, Davina Bhandar, Renisa Mawani, and Satwinder Kaur Bains

White Fragility: Why It's So Hard for White People to Talk about Racism by Robin DiAngelo

Another Politics: Talking across Today's Transformative Movements by Chris Dixon

The Souls of Black Folk by W.E.B. Du Bois

The Birth of Territory by Stuart Elden

The Black Book of Canadian Foreign Policy by Yves Engler

Canada in Haiti: Waging War on the Poor Majority by Yves Engler and Anthony Fenton

Behind the Police three-episode series on *Behind the Bastards* podcast (globalplayer.com/podcasts/2T3Bh) by Robert Evans

Black Skin, White Masks by Frantz Fanon

The Wretched of the Earth by Frantz Fanon

Claiming Anishinaabe: Decolonizing the Human Spirit by Lynn Gehl

The Truth that Wampum Tells: My Debwewin on the Algonquin Land Claims Process by Lynn Gehl

Let's Talk Race: A Guide for White People by Fern L. Johnson and Marlene G. Fine

Abolitionist Intimacies by El Jones

Live from the Afrikan Resistance! by El Jones

500 Hundred Years of Indigenous Resistance by Gord Hill

The Black Jacobins: Toussaint L'Ouverture and the San Domingo Revolution by C.L.R. James

You Don't Play with Revolution by C.L.R James

The Imagination of the New Left: A Global Analysis of 1968 by George Katsiaficas

How to Be an Antiracist by Ibram X. Kendi

"Decolonizing Anti-Racism" (shorturl.at/ilPU5) by Bonita Lawrence and Enakshi Dua

Why Race Still Matters by Alana Lentin

Distorted Descent: White Claims to Indigenous Identity by Darryl Leroux

The Many-Headed Hydra: Sailors, Slaves, Commoners, and the Hidden History of the Revolutionary Atlantic by Peter Linebaugh and Marcus Rediker

The Master's Tools Will Never Dismantle the Master's House by Audre Lorde

Unsettled Expectations: Uncertainty, Land and Settler Decolonization by Eva Mackey

Neither Settler nor Native: The Making and Unmaking of Permanent Minorities by Mahmood Mamdani

My Conversations with Canadians by Lee Maracle

Policing Black Lives: State Violence in Canada from Slavery to the Present by Robyn Maynard

Republic of Lies: American Conspiracy Theorists and Their Surprising Rise to Power by Anna Merlan

The White Possessive: Property, Power, and Indigenous Sovereignty by Aileen Moreton-Robinson

Documentaries by Alanis Obomsawin available on the National Film Board website (nfb.ca)

The History of White People by Nell Irvin Painter

We Were Not the Savages: Collision between European and Native American Civilizations by Daniel N. Paul

Take d Milk, Nah? by Jivesh Parasram

The Darker Nations: A People's History of the Third World by Vijay Prashad

Looking White People in the Eye: Gender, Race, and Culture in Courtrooms and Classrooms by Sherene Razack

The Groundings with My Brothers by Walter Rodney

How Europe Underdeveloped Africa by Walter Rodney

Colored White: Transcending the Racial Past by David R. Roediger

Working towards Whiteness: How America's Immigrants Became White by David R. Roediger

Displacing Blackness: Planning, Power, and Race in Twentieth-Century Halifax by Ted Rutland

Orientalism by Edward Said

Against the Grain: A Deep History of the Earliest States by James C. Scott

The Art of Not Being Governed: An Anarchist History of Upland Southeast Asia by James C. Scott

Seeing Like a State: How Certain Schemes to Improve the Human Condition Have Failed by James C. Scott

"Race and Revolution at Bwa Kayiman," *Millennium: Journal of International Studies*, by Robbie Shilliam

Canada in the World: Settler Capitalism and the Colonial Imagination by Tyler Shipley

As We Have Always Done: Indigenous Freedom through Radical Resistance by Leanne Betasamosake Simpson

"The Brilliance of the Beaver: Learning from an Anishnaabe World," (https://www.cbc.ca/player/play/1725600323622) audio lecture by Leanne Betasamosake Simpson

Lighting the Eighth Fire: The Liberation, Resurgence, and Protection of Indigenous Nations by Leanne Betasamosake Simpson

Inglorious Empire: What the British Did to India by Shashi Tharoor

Exalted Subjects: Studies in the Making of Race and Nation in Canada by Sunera Thobani

Is Free Speech Racist? by Gavan Titley

The Settler Colonial Present by Lorenzo Veracini

The End of Policing by Alex S. Vitale

White World Order, Black Power Politics: The Birth of American International Relations by Robert Vitalis

Border and Rule: Global Migration, Capitalism, and the Rise of Racist Nationalism by Harsha Walia

Undoing Border Imperialism by Harsha Walia

Insurgent Love: Abolition and Domestic Homicide by Ardath Whynacht

Capitalism and Slavery by Eric Williams

Thinking Orientals: Migration, Contact, and Exoticism in Modern America by Henry Yu

Blood and Politics: The History of the White Nationalist Movement from the Margins to the Mainstream by Leonard Zeskind

ACKNOWLEDGEMENTS

Ajay: It takes a lot of work to talk about heavy stuff like this in a light way, but writing this book was an exercise in mutual aid and community care. My great appreciation to Alex Khasnabish and Fazeela Jiwa, without whom there would have been no episodes or book. I am grateful also for the conversations, perspectives, trust, and writings on this subject from El Jones, Candida Hadley, Matthew Hayes, Jon Langdon, Daniel Tubb, Ardath Whynacht, Sharri Plonski, and Lisa Tilley. I appreciate the work of the research assistants and transcribers who supported this work, including Courtney Law, Liam Patrick, Raymond Moylan, and Leah Horlick. I am grateful to Fernwood Publishing for the outstanding support for this book, and to Erin Seatter for her politically informed copyediting skills. I also acknowledge the trust and comradery of students who have helped shape my thinking on race and our current predicament in Canada: Masuma Khan, Caleigh Wong, Amaan Kazmi, Madison Gateman, Mercedes Peters, Fatima Beydoun, Claudia Castillo-Prentt, Madeleine Gan, and Selam Abdella. Many thanks also to the hundreds of people who have posed questions through SSFWQ episodes over the last two years, and to the hundreds of informants (some white, some not) who have sharpened my analysis on this subject over the years. Finally, I am grateful to be permitted to make a home in Mi'kma'ki and hope these efforts to create some starting points for dismantling structural white supremacy will be of service to Mi'kmaq, African Nova Scotians, and all people striving to find a better way to live in the colonial present. This book is for Ayaan, in hopes that she will grow up differently than her old man did.

Alex: I'm deeply grateful to my accomplices in all of this: Ajay Parasram, Fazeela Jiwa, and Candida Hadley. Thanks to all the staff at Fernwood Publishing who helped bring this book into the world and to those who took the time to read and respond to it so we could try to make it better. This book is for my kids, Indra and Eshan, and all those like them, who deserve a better future than the one looming before us. This book is dedicated to all the race traitors, rebels, radicals, and revolutionaries who keep the struggle for collective liberation alive.